WORKERS CITY

With an Introduction and Notes by
FARQUHAR McLAY

1988
Clydeside Press (Publishing) Ltd.
37 High Street
Glasgow

Acknowledgements:

MacMillan, London Ltd. for extract from 'Wisdom, Madness and Folly' by R. D. Laing.
Fat Cat Publications for 'The Orra Man' from 'At Glasgow Cross and Other Poems' by Freddie Anderson.

We have sought where possible full permission to include the material chosen in WORKERS CITY. The editor and publishers apologise for any error or omission, either textual or attributive, and will be pleased to receive further information regarding any author or passage selected in this anthology.

Contents

The Scottish literary tradition is quite clear. You speak out for the people all the time. It is a people's tradition. Whoever or whatever happens to coincide with the people's tradition, you back them up and you don't split hairs. That's how you keep with the thing. Solidarity without compromise.

Thurso Berwick

Drumchapel engulfed them like quicksand.
'Some place,' Laidlaw said.
'Aye, there must be some terrible people here.'
'No', Laidlaw said. 'That's not what I mean. I find the people very impressive. It's the place that's terrible. You think of Glasgow. At each of its four corners, this kind of housing-scheme. There's the Drum and Easterhouse and Pollok and Castlemilk. You've got the biggest housing-scheme in Europe here. And what's there? Hardly anything but houses. Just architectural dumps where they unloaded the people like slurry. Penal architecture. Glasgow folk have to be nice people. Otherwise, they would have burned the place to the ground years ago.'

William McIlvanney, 'Laidlaw'

INTRODUCTION *by Farquhar McLay*

GLASGOW: EUROPEAN CITY of Culture 1990. The announcement came from the Tory Arts minister, Edward Luce, in October 1986. It had a sickeningly hollow ring to it. Looking at the social, cultural and economic deprivation in working-class areas of Glasgow, and thinking about the rigours of the new Social Fund and Poll Tax to come, it sounded like blatant and cynical mockery. And indeed a wry smile was the most usual reaction when people bothered to take the slightest notice. And not many did. Even with the massive hype given to it in the capitalist press, most people took it as just another EEC/Tory con trick. It was hard to see it as anything else. One thought immediately of The Babbity Bowster and town-centre homes for yuppies. Of the new Sheriff Court, the largest in Europe, with cell space in its bowels for 2,000 prisoners *in emergencies.* Of the Scottish judiciary which imprisons a higher proportion of the population than any European country except Turkey. (There were 13 deaths in Scottish prisons in 1987 alone.) Of Strathclyde's 200,000 unemployed (whatever the Government's current distortion of the true figure might be) and the close to 8,000 classified homeless (with council waiting lists up by 34% in the last five years).

In the light of the hard facts of life as it is lived by people at the bottom of the heap in Glasgow, it is difficult to see the 'culture' tag as being anything other than a sham accolade to help grease the wheels of capitalist enterprise and smooth the path for the politicians. It is little wonder working-class Glasgow remains unimpressed. There is widespread acceptance that it has nothing whatever to do with the working- or the workless-class poor of Glasgow but everything to do with big business and money: to pull in investment for inner-city developments which, in the obsessive drive to make the centre of the city attractive to tourists, can only work to the further disadvantage of the people in the poverty ghettoes on the outskirts. The so-called Merchant City might be reborn but only for those and such as those: the well-heeled who serve and perpetuate the system and profit by the miseries and inequalities inherent in the system: the kind of people who now find themselves installed in central areas where the have-nots "who have not yet benefited from the Thatcher revolution" were long ago uprooted. The rest is just camouflage. Like the million pound spend annually maintaining security at the Burrell whilst housing-scheme squalor gets a pittance. Like the Regional Council laying out £62,000 to stone-clean the Talbot Centre's exterior whilst the residents within still kip on the floor. That is your Culture City in a nutshell.

Of course it is no new thing for the city authorities to be in the camouflage business. They were in the same business in the 1920s, shouting about 'libels on

Glasgow', when it would have taxed an ingenious mind to invent a libel more outrageous than the reality prevailing at the time. Yet contemprorary accounts of life in working-class Glasgow in the 20-year period 1915-1935 were by no means widespread. Two of the frankest, and indeed the best known, are William Bolitho's essay *Cancer of Empire* which is a vivid factual presentation (revealingly enough, by an Englishman) of the truth as he found it, and later on McArthur and Long's *No Mean City* which would work roughly the same appalling social conditions into fiction. They were certainly an improvement on the mushy idylls of the kailyairders. Both books can be read as harrowing indictments of the power elite in Scotland who administered the country more or less as a colony of England, presiding with brutal insensitivity over mass poverty and disease and the highest infant mortality rate in Western Europe. Sadly, however, no Scottish poet, novelist or playwright (or even historian until fairly recent date) was able to resist the political and cultural dominance of London in sufficient degree to be able to depict, in its savage and unsentimental totality, the only real challenge to this rampant capitalist oppression: the class war in Glasgow.

For alongside the poverty and disease and wasted lives there was the glory and heroism of those who resolutely engaged reaction and put Glasgow in the vanguard of revolution, not just here in these islands but throughout the world. The men and women who rejected parliamentary opportunism and sought to advance the people's struggle in the work-place and in the streets. The trials for treason and sedition which mark Glasgow's history tell their own story. It is a story which continues into our own day. It is not a libel on Glasgow but her vindication. The lies and hypocrisy of mealy-mouthed councillors and turncoat Reds can change nothing of that. Nor can the cheap trickery of PR frauds blind us to the evils of the present. For although modes of repression and control in State bureaucracies may have changed, relying today as much on advertising conmanship as on police coercion, and although the new capitalist-controlled computer technologies exploit and impoverish and degrade us in ways which were hardly imaginable even fifty years ago, yet it is still repression for all that, it is still exploitation, it is still impoverishment, and it is still degradation. The stark evidence of the peripheral housing schemes makes that abundantly clear.

Working-class Glasgow is for the most part de-industrialised Glasgow. De-industrialised Glasgow is living in a distant scheme, without amenity and without community, and waiting for the Giro.

In the long term, waiting for the Giro must lead to social sterility, with all the outlets for creative social involvement blocked off, and tine not for making in and growing in but filled only with unrelieved waiting, like the prisoner without a release date.

The damaging impact on people's health, physically and psychologically, is well known. Indeed it says a great deal for the resilience of spirit and character in the unemployed population that social and psychological distortions are not even more prevalent than we see today.

But one thing is certain. The situation as it exists today is admirably suited for the effective control and administration of the population. The demoralised working class is without muscle, without mobility in any direction except down, and has even been robbed of its own authentic voice. Communications technology, particularly television, owned and controlled by the multi-nationals and the State, makes this a simpler task than in the past. The renowned working-class social-cultural cohesion and shopfloor solidarity have been largely smashed by the break-up of the tenement communities and the terror of mass unemployment. Progressive strains in working-class culture are everywhere being vitiated. In our de-socialised neo-technical age the political bureaucracy, through the mass media, is able to assimilate and render benign most forms of popular disaffection. In post-TV politics even protest which has honest intent can easily become something very like complicity.

And whilst working-class Glasgow is in a kind of death, middle-class Glasgow is in the throes of regeneration. The Labour Council knows where it stands. There is no capitalist enterprise that will not be looked upon favourably if it comes under scrutiny for a grant. Come on, they tell us, play the game. The wine-bar economy is all we've got and it's blossoming, so don't start knocking it for Christ's sake. No more libels on Glasgow, please! Scottish Tourist Board Chairman, Mr Devereux: "The city's spectacular renaissance has put it in the premier league of tourist destinations worldwide." This is the acme of bourgeois progress: after two centuries of brutal industrialism, with all its miserable corruption and destructiveness in terms of human life and the living environment, they can make welders in waiters!

And not that anybody is forgetting art. To be embraced as the Cultural Capital of Europe, succeeding Florence, Athens and Paris, you have to have art: that is to say, lots of imported music, opera and ballet, sepulchral museums, high-priced paintings and a civic theatre devoted solely to classics – pale ghosts of revolt in other places, at other times – in a word, the kind of art that is no real threat to the social reality of the present, the kind of art that can work no change in the here-and-now because its time has passed and its place is not the here-and-now.

It can teach us one thing though. Art to be valid in its own day must be in revolt against the official mirage of its own day: against the impossibility of freedom in its own day.

Its true and essential dynamic is always and everywhere revolt. The art of the past has no more splendid message to disclose. It is this and only this which gives it life and value in another age. But it is not a transferrable dynamic. Each age must find its own and battle the received absurdity anew. The art of the past, now a safe commodity, lends itself easily to resurrection and celebration. Here and there it may indeed still bring genuine inspiration and delight. But mostly it manifests itself as just another facet of oppression, simply adding to the meaninglessness of life and work in the social-political-economic irrationality of the present, and serving only to stabilise officially sanctioned values.

This is not to deny the power and value of tradition but to catch at its very essence. If you make it an altar at which its passive devotees kneel and do homage, as with the Burns cult for example, you'd be as well in the cemetery with a heap of old bones. What is vital for us in tradition is not merely, as we are so often told, that it is *our* past, but that we make certain the same spark that once gave it life can be struck anew by us to give us life in our own time. Otherwise it is just a cloying encumbrance, a nostalgic wank, an academic pastime. It should speak to us of resistance to the official fakery of the State in all its manifold forms (even if it is only to invent a fakery of our own but one that opens up the world for all the people everywhere and gives our best and most creative energies the possibility of fulfilment); it should speak to us of revolt against the oxbow authority has yoked us in, in body as well as in spirit, where we stand duped by fear and distrust of our own selves, fit only for eager subservience and our only song a hosanna to hierarchy; and it should speak to us of the one struggle worthy of every man and woman today, as it has been throughout all ages past – the struggle for the ultimate social, cultural and economic integrity of all humankind.

This anthology is testimony to that response, past and present, in and around Glasgow and its people. Naturally it is far from being the complete story – no one book could be that. It must necessarily be a hint merely – but a hint which ought to be both illuminating and inspirational – of the liberating power of working-class experience and consciousness in a long-standing tradition of struggle.

It is a tradition which the establishment and the media like to romanticise into caricature historically, but at the same time root out, castigate and belittle in the contemporary scene. For it is a tradition which re-emerges defiantly with every new generation. It is the tradition of working-class people refusing to be passive and cowed and mute, compliant victims of the political bureaucracy and all agog for the Westminster charade. It is the tradition of grassroots solidarity and total distrust of power and officialdom: of uncompromising resistance to the State's authority in every sphere of life and no matter who is weilding it. It is in this tradition all social, economic and political advancement of working-class people originally took seed. It is here with us now. It is a seed the people in power would like to see trampled underfoot forever, for they, better than anybody, know its potency as a weapon against them. And needing our co-operation and trust as much as they do, they would persuade us to look elsewhere for our betterment. Too often we have and always with the same shameful and disastrous results. That is the one incontestable fact in the history of the working classes. Surely it is time we stopped looking elsewhere. The answer is here now.

ANNE MULLEN

To Whom It May Concern

I read about it in the papers, I'm seeing it
on the news. COME TO GLASGOW THE CULTURE CITY.
.... It's giving me the blues.

COME TO GLASGOW'S GARDEN FESTIVAL. Only one
week's buroo money. We could live off the smell
of flowers. While they reap all the money.

ENTERTAINMENT CITY. To the exclusive few.
40 grand houses, a shopping mall, an opera
house or two. ENTERTAINMENT CITY ....
For who?

William needs new shoes, the window's needing
fixed, the roof is letting in water and the
settee's needing stitched.

Can you read between the lines. Have you ever
really tried.... Don't you really want to know
what it is they're trying to hide.

JANETTE SHEPHARD

Where I Came From

WHAT A DIRTY, smelly, insanitary place the Gorbals must have been when I was a child, and yet, knowing nothing else, we accepted it.

The old tenement building had three families each floor and shared a toilet.

The family next door had thirteen members. So, it appeared at times it was their toilet with the constant queue. Of course, everybody had a pot in the house for emergencies. There were some very old shops beside us. All dirty, dusty and musty. I remember being a bit frightened in some of them, as the ancient shop-keepers seemed a part of the shop with their dusty appearance. One, I remember, was a very small stair lady. She constantly sniffed and her nose was all brown from taking snuff. She kept her pot behind the counter. She shuffled along, wheezing and sniffing and I waged a battle with myself, telling myself I wasn't afraid of her.

Dirty Maggie's on the other side of the road was nearly as bad, but at least she didn't wheeze and sniff. She had bad eyes and white straight hair. A better witch I've never seen. She dealt in comics and books, so it didn't matter how filthy her shop was (and it was), at least you didn't have to eat her products. My brothers were comics mad and I usually made quite a few trips a day changing their comics for them.

We played in the back court sometimes. Digging in the dirt and, if it rained, we made mud pies and had great fun in the puddles. We played at shops and used stones and broken glass for money. We walked along and climbed the dykes round all the backs, often a good height, and I often felt a bit dizzy, but no one was allowed to be afraid in the Gorbals.

In the streets the games were numerous. Skipping ropes, ball games, whip and peerie, even old tin cans on strings and you walked about on them. Now and again a roller skate would appear and we would all have a shot, strapped to your foot with a string or an old tie. I never dreamt that skates came in pairs.

The running games were great fun. Tig, and 'kick door run fast', but someone always got caught and you were told on and landed in trouble.

We never saw much grass or flowers and it was a novelty to roll on grass and pick flowers and, visiting even Gran who had a garden, was a real treat. Gran had a four-apartment house and a bathroom and I personally thought they were toffs that lived in that mansion.

At school, well, that was a serious business, and you sat up straight, arms folded learnt your tables and always had a long, sharp pencil 'or else'. The teacher did an inspection every day, so it was best to have clean hands and face. Clean teeth and shoes and your hair combed to be safe.

My two brothers and my sister and I shared a room. The boys had an inset bed and we had a bed settee. They would tell us ghost stories at night and then frighten us by creeping about in the dark and touching our hands or face. Dad and mum and my baby brother slept in the kitchen in an inset bed. A small hall, and that was our home.

How the lot next door managed is a mystery. We had an old black grate with the fire at the front, but it wasn't used for cooking as we had a gas cooker. Sunday was bath night and it took all night, by the time the large zinc bath was dragged out and relieved of the weekly washing it held. Then dad and mum proceeded to fill it up with hot water heated in pots and kettles. It was youngest first and I was glad I didn't have to get washed after my dirty big brothers. Most of the washing was done at the laundry, but some could hang on a string at the mantlepiece and be dried by the fire. There was a pole with string threaded through and it could hold the baby's nappies to be dried outside the window. The weekend was a good laugh and we would all hang out the window watching all the men coming out of the pubs. One on each corner of the street. There would be squabbles that would be more funny than serious. We could spot our dad a mile away, as his hands would be everywhere describing everything he was speaking about. Mum would laugh and say without his hands he would be dumb.

We didn't lead a typical Gorbals life, as our father was a hard worker and always got good jobs in the chemical factory he worked in, and carried coal when he was laid off work. So, we were always well fed and clothed. We were the first to have a T.V. in our area and our house was full for months, till all the neighbours got to see the telly.

I was eleven when I was told we were moving to Castlemilk. Some far off place I'd never heard of. So we moved lock stock and barrel. All the family except mum and I had the flu' and the baby had pneumonia. It was December 13th – wonder why I remember! All our things got soaked and had to be dried and it was some time before we got our beds organised. It was freezing cold, although our fire blazed up the chimney. It was very draughty, all those doors and windows, but it was so exciting, all this space, even if for a moment we were all huddled in the living room where it was warmest. The bathroom was a delight and no queue either, there was even hot running water. Oh, this was heaven. Looking out the windows onto the beautiful white wilderness was wonderful. It was so clean, the air so fresh, there were even trees and we were facing a golf course. My sister and I got to sleep on our bed settee in the living room to keep us warm that winter, but later on we shared a room and it was great. We had a small electric fire and a record player and dad bought us a small bedroom suite and fitted carpet. Oh, weren't we toffs. Life was entirely different. It was a distance to the shops and we had to travel to school and dad had to get a bike as there was no buses for his early shift. That first summer was glorious and all the children knew each other by then, we were all in the same boat and had left our old pals behind. We all seemed to cling together, boys and girls, and went about in a big gang exploring all the woods and fields. There was even a river and we had a great time building fires to keep us warm after playing in the water and singing songs round it. We often overstayed our bed times and our mums would be there to meet us with a skelp for being late. Our lifestyle had changed but it seemed mums hadn't changed at all.

Sunday mass was like a real trek and it was more like mountain-climbing than walking. It was a distance away and we sometimes got lost. It was held in a wooden hut and it was very small and the children sat on the floor. That was very strange. My best friend moved back to the Gorbals and I used to visit her and stay sometimes and it was great fun. Us being older then, I saw it differently. It had much more life than Castlemilk. All the best-looking boys stayed in the Gorbals and we would meet them out for walks and have a chat. The town and the barrows were within walking distance from the Gorbals, but I would only have to step off the 'bus going home and breathe in the beautiful clean air and be glad I was home. In latter years I loved to bring my child up in such healthy surroundings. The lovely parks we have where children can play in safety and just to see the healthy glow. Well none of us Gorbals lot looked like that!

The healthy glow is still in the children of Castlemilk, but now the promised land is rather tarnished. Dampness problems are widespread causing misery. Solvent and drug abuse spreading daily. Neglect showing everywhere, unemployment is just another daily topic. The hopelessness is everywhere, people are giving in and, just when we needed it most, a shiny new pub at the shopping centre. No doubt so we can all drown our sorrows in drink and blur the vision we come home to.

Maybe there will be another Castlemilk someday, but I hope it lives up more to its promises than this one did.

Christmas Party

SHE HAD JUST about had it. Soaked to the skin. Julie and David clinging to each side of the buggy, Susan wailing inside. All soaked and freezing for nothing. Approaching their close Julie took David's hand to run on. It took him so long climbing the three flights of stairs to their home.

Home, she thought. A freezing damp hole. Last year the round of officials had been soul-destroying. Doctor's letters proving their children's health was at risk to no avail. With "points points points" ringing in her ears she had given up. Sick of getting messed about waiting in queues, only to be left in floods of tears at the injustice of it all. They had slipped beneath the world's notice now. Dirty and shabby – no-one listened.

Today at the social security had been more of the same: no clothing allowance. Only once a year was allowed. Stuttering to deaf ears that the summer clothing was washed out and inadequate as she could see from the blue shivering children. No heating allowance: they had £1.10 already. No linen or blankets; she'd had them too. The stuttering voice explained about bed-wetting, broken washing machine. The cold house.

As the young girl glanced at her watch Margaret got to her feet. The girl didn't understand, like herself maybe at that age. No time for dirty beggars. Like always she cried. For the young girl gone. Was she really only 25. Memories of her handsome husband flooding her mind and eyes. He'd got them in this mess and then walked out. No-one told her she wasn't liable for his debts and she'd struggled – leaving them short to pay his bills for clothes and furniture he'd insisted they needed. Leaving had spared him seeing it all re-possessed. Scarring her forever with shame.

Exhausted on reaching the top landing, glad to set the buggy down. She wasn't too well these days. Julie and David had shed their anoraks. She laughed at them sitting in front of the fire and plugged it in, two bars for a while to heat the house a little. They needed a hot drink. She put the kettle on before she attended to Susan. Too tired to wail – now just whimpering. She put some tea in her bottle, not enough milk yet again.

Julie helped David into his pyjamas as their mother stripped the baby and changed her nappy. A lump rose in her throat at little Julie not yet five playing mother for real. Susan was asleep half way through her bottle. The good thing about the bed in the living-room – now she didn't wake on impact with the cold covers like in the bedroom. They kept each other warm all huddled in one bed.

Night was worse for her with the children asleep her mind clawed over the last three torturous years – no wonder she didn't sleep much. Trying to tell the doctor she couldn't take sleeping tablets with three young children was useless. The bathroom held umpteen bottles – tried and abandoned. She'd seen the look on the health visitor's face and the attendance officer as she slurred her confused words at them. She didn't open the door to them now. That was all the visitors they ever had. Julie had been sent home to change her canvas shoes she had got soaked. She had no others. So shame had kept her home for two weeks. She'd hardly been at school since her enrolement a few months before. Plagued by colds and coughs.

John, her brother, said he might pop in this week. She knew he wouldn't. She had seen him last week almost cross the road to avoid them, then changed his mind. Always handsome – like her twin she had been told. Not now though. Beautifully dressed like always he patted Julie's head like she had scabies. They all had the cold and runny red noses. A sign he wouldn't be used to. He should have walked by. It made her feel worse. He had done it before only she never let on she had seen him either.

Depression was taking a real hold on her now. Making the children cosy and comfortable had given her some satisfaction. Now she was so short of money she couldn't even make them decent meals or dress them warmly – no wonder Tony had gone off – she was useless. Christmas was only a few weeks away. No toys this year. At least there was no constant reminder since the TV was reclaimed.

Sitting up just used electricity. So she lay down in the dark beside her children staring into space. It seemed she had just shut her eyes when the post fell to the floor. Dragging herself up, hoping for some good news from someone. Maybe Tony coming back. She smiled at the thought; he would hardly recognise her now. The electricity bill. She couldn't believe it – £125! An official letter. Tony had applied for a divorce. Swaying up the hall; a cup of coffee she thought. No milk – oh shit! She fell into a chair and sobbed her heart out.

Dry-eyed now, she washed her face and fetched a carrier bag and her purse. It held £3. The corner shop would be opened now. Back home with her purchases; six pints of milk, a loaf, a tin of hot chocolates and three small bars of chocolate. They would think it was Christmas. She made a plate of jam sandwiches and put a large pot of milk on the heat for chocolate. The living room was heating up nicely – two bars and the convector on too. Never had so much electricity flowed through the fire before. Giggling that she wouldn't be paying for it. Checking the strongest sleeping tablets she shook them into the milk, seeing them dissolve then pouring more in. Stirring almost half a tin of chocolate into the mixture then tasting it. Umm, lovely, she thought.

Time the children were up for their party. They needed the radio on as well. The neighbours next door banged the wall almost immediately. She turned the radio louder. The only time she saw her was for complaints. Her turn of the stairs. The children were noisy. Margaret had been silly enough to ask her for some milk a few weeks ago when Susan was ill and couldn't settle. She had refused and Margaret had seen her shopping bag with four pints that morning. It really hurt. She never borrowed and would have given it back. She was like a lot of people upset at poverty on TV and ignored it under their nose.

The noise awoke the children. Bewildered until they spied the sandwiches and chocolate. They all tucked in like it was cream cakes. The hot chocolate delighted them too. Margaret topped the mugs with cold milk as it was too warm for them. Susan had a bottle full and loved it. They danced and played games. This was the old Mummy Julie knew and she was so happy. Maybe Daddy would come back too. The mugs of chocolate were refilled as soon as they finished. Their tummys were bursting but they loved the warm sweet drink.

One by one Margaret tucked them up in bed lovingly kissing and cuddling them in turn.

She sat with the last mug of chocolate and turned the fire down. Laughing hysterically that it was too warm. She crawled into the bed beside the children.

That was the scene when they broke the door down. John had called a few times with bags of messages, not got in and got worried when the health visitor said she didn't let her in now either. The young policeman wept unashamedly. John stood like a zombie with his shopping bags. The older policeman went through the mail that lay behind the door. Nothing important – only bills and a social security letter stating a visitor was calling.

The young girl had patched up the fight with her boyfriend. She'd been fed up the day the woman came in to the office. Later that night she felt guilty at how poor and frozen they had looked and next morning decided to check if she was entitled to anything and found that she was.

She would be pleased to receive her letter – poor soul.

WILLIAM SUTHERLAND

fae *A Clydeside Lad*

The clackity boots hit the cobbildy stanes
   an thir faces wir mawkit wae greeze;
wae thir laughin an jokin an wavin tae wains
   they were giants in blue dungarees.

An staunin ootside wae her aperon on
   wis the wee nebby frame o ma mither
an she nodded tae Joe an she nodded tae John
   bit her eyes keepin skint fur anither.

Fur last night wis poor an we huid tae make dae
   wae breid an a bit o a bridie
bit we'll aw hiv fish an some totties the day
   fur Da's comin hame an it's Friday.

So Maw's staunin ther, is we play bae the drains,
   an we're waitin an waitin fur ages,
bit the clackity boots on the cobbildy stanes
   tell us Da's comin hame wae the wages.

A thrupenny bit wis the usual Ah got
   bit wan time when Ah got a tanner
Ah ran roon tae Woolies' an ther whit Ah bought
   wis some toty wee bolts and a SPANNER!

Fur the fitters, the jiners, the men fae the cranes,
   the labourirs, clerks, engineers,
an the clack o thir boots on the cobbildy stanes
   wance rang like a song in ma ears.

      *   *   *

Whit bitter feelins gnaw an freeze us
is in these wids noo on ma tod
Ah groan like pain-wrackt, faithliss Jesus
up tae a faur an frozen God.

Fur jist this day we buried Ann,
struck doon an taken bae TB
an the priest said his "Remember, man..."
ower a deid wain o only three.

Bit whit's TB? It's jist a name
fur waas thit breathe oot damp, an hum
wae mould, an turn a wid-be hame
intae a dank and stinkin slum.

It's jist the name fur poverty
thit breks the will o decent mithers
an makes sae flyly, gradjilly,
auld drunkirds oot o wid-be fethirs.

TB's the word thit doctors gie
tae factirs fur tae hide behin,
tae aw the world so no tae see
the breadth an depth o their ain sin.

Bit, Ann, lass, you wir aye sae thin,
yer lips sae pale, yer skin sae drawn,
it seemt aroon ye fae within
a powerfu, daithly beauty shone.

God curse ye, daith, then, thit ye sher
wae love an health the power tae gie
the human face a comely er
an light it up, like tenderly!

An God tae, aye, God, whit o you
tae act is if yer hauns ir tied
an staun back watchin is anew
an innacint is crucified...

Bit look here noo, afore ma feet
wan tiny snowdrap grows apert
an glows sae lonely an sae sweet
Ah fear it tae will brek ma hert.

Aw Man, God says, ye ir bit grass
thit lives an dies inside an hoor;
bit Ann, Ah says, wee breathliss lass
ye ir this toty snowdrap-flooer

thit lives oot in the winds an snows
an smiles up it the winter's sting
an dies afore it ever knows
the waarmin sun an smir o Spring.

Bit, lass, ye've sown two seed fur sure,
two seeds tae grauw an bide in me –
the sadniss o the snowdrap-flooer,
an the blasphemy o poverty.

*   *   *

Now standing on this driftwood-line,
here time itself feels in suspension;
here only memories are mine,
big, broken things it hurts to mention.

For politics that hymn a war
eight thousand shameless miles away
are well content with dirges for
this river that once served their day.

An arc-light flashing down the Clyde
recalls again my town of old;
yet just this day too Greenock's pride
was bought and sold for English gold.

But wheesht! There! did you hear the river,
this tide that turns in us as deep,
shake off the moment with a shiver
and turn, a giant in its sleep...

BRENDAN McLAUGHLIN

Life's a Bowl a' Cherries

"AW JESUS THERE'S the whistle," Jimmy cursed to himself as he ran towards the platform gate.

"Is that the Johnstone train?"

The ticket collector muttered, "Ye're too late noo son it's away" just as Jimmy vaulted the fence beside the closed gate.

"Heh, whit's the score you. Did you see that, Alec? Christ this joab wid burst yer heid sometimes."

"It wisnae the joab thit wis burstin' yer heid last night Sammy," laughed his mate, "Aye ye were nae picture yersel' then."

Jimmy just managed to open the door of the rearmost carriage of the train as it rumbled away from the platform gasping for breath, his head back against the toilet door, he sighed with the relief that he would be on time for his work.

In the reluctant comfort of this thought, he relaxed against the door which clicked and sprung open pitching him inwards into the startled embrace of the man who had just been coming out of the toilet.

"Jesus Christ," exclaimed Jimmy as the man caught him.

"Naw but ye'd think Ah wis, the way you're fallin ower yersel' for me."

"Don't be funny," Jimmy blasted. "Ye shouldnie'uv been usin' the toilet anyway when the train's in the station. Look, there's the notice."

"Heh you're in a right mood, son," the man said as he struggled past Jimmy leaving him the sole occupant of the toilet. As he was leaving the toilet he caught a glimpse of himself in the mirror and saw that his face was flushed. "Christ that cannae be me, ah'm only twenty-two an' that face in there looks like it's git wan foot in the grave."

Desperate for a seat and a smoke, breathlessly he struggled along the overcrowded carriages. "British effin' Rail," Jimmy uttered as he entered the last carriage. "Surely the boays'll be in here."

Right enough, there they were, four of them, fully occupying the four seats across the passageway from the only vacant seat in the carriage.

"Thank Christ a seat at last," Jimmy thought as he acknowledged his workmates with an exasperated nod.

On the vacant seat lay a pair of black leather gloves and Jimmy hesitated expectantly before saying, "Excuse me, Jim, are they your gloves?"

A well groomed head looked over the top of the Glasgow Herald and indifferently replied, "Yes".

"Could you possibly move them so thit ah can sit down please," asked Jimmy.

"Are you sure that you are in the correct compartment young man," enquired the voice.

"Well it's certainly no' a glove compartment, so gonny move them."

"Have you got a first class ticket in your possession," demanded the voice.

"Hiv you got wan?" snarled Jimmy, abandoning any attempt to be courteous.

"Of course I have," said the voice becoming indignant and making a sweeping gesture with its arm, "but I doubt if you, or these, would have."

In a state of affrontery and anger, Jimmy picked the gloves up from the seat, threw them at the voice's face and defiantly sat down beside its perplexed astonishment.

"I shall report you to the guard," assured the voice. "I demand to see your ticket."

"I demand tae see yours first," retorted Jimmy, "show me it."

"I most certainly will not," replied the voice, "you are not in the least part entitled to see my ticket."

"That's right," gasped Jimmy, "an' you're no' entitled tae see mine either so shut it an' get on wi' yer paper."

"You can rest assured I will be taking this further," insisted the voice.

"Aye tae Paisley and Largs," smirked Jimmy with a triumphant sneer as he turned to his workmates to discover that he was being totally ignored.

As the train sped through the Hillington stations, it was as if it exuded a sense of arrogant pride in the security that it continued to run back and forth between Glasgow and Largs, insensitive to the accumulated closures which were occuring on the Industrial Estate that these railway stations served. As if the boarded-up emptiness of the estate caused the passengers on the train to silently ponder their own personal futures, the tense atmosphere seemed to dissolve as it was absorbed by the different people.

Jimmy searched in his pockets for the packet of cigarettes which he'd bought at Central Station but could not find them.

"Jesus Christ, they must've fell oot mah pocket when Ah jumped that fence."

He leaned over to his mates, "heh, Raymie len' me a fag, jist till we get tae Johnstone."

The cigarette was thrown over to Jimmy and he had to snatch it out of the air snapping it in two. He lit the half with the filter on it and put the other half in his pocket.

When he attempted to use the ashtray he annoyingly found he could not, as it was being covered by a pinstriped terylene sleeve, a protruding white cuff with gold personalised links and a wafer thin gold watch.

The hand at the end of this ensemble was holding the newspaper right across the divider – well into the area in front of Jimmy.

"Would ye mind shiftin' ye'r paper, ah'd like tae use the ashtray."

With an affected cough, the man thrust his arm even further across Jimmy's space.

At this gesture, Jimmy seemed to relax, sat back, looking at his mates – and with a wry twist on his mouth, pushed the lit cigarette towards the ashtray which of course came to rest on the pin-striped sleeve. A few seconds later, the pungent smell of scorched terylene alerted the gentleman as well as everyone else in the carriage, that something was not right.

On realising that the smell was emanating from his own sleeve, the prim personage violently came to life, drew his arm in horror and proceeded to get into the most outrageous fankle, knocking his spectacles off then accidently treading the usefulness out of them as they lay on the floor. His carefully cultivated equanimity asunder, he screeched: "My syoot, my syoot, you have ruined my syoot!" and as he discovered that his spectacles were lying broken on the floor, "my spectacles my..." and as he bent down to pick them up, "oh my head," as his head met with the table edge.

"This is criminal assault, you, you Glaswegian lout. You will pay for this. I am going to have you arrested. Your kind are all the same."

The wee woman sitting across from Jimmy wailed, "Aw Jesus, he'll get us aw the jeyal."

When the train slid to a halt at Paisley, the besyooted, pin-stripped man left the train and returned with a policeman.

The policeman asked to see Jimmy's ticket and was scrutinising its validity when he was urged to pursue the complaint of assault, and to "have the lout removed from the train and charged accordingly. Forthwith."

The policeman didn't seem to know what to do when his indecision was relieved by the lilting accent of an Irishman wearing an old bunnet, a brown pinstriped suit and wellies. "Well ye see now, Sergeant, dough I wud never be the one to tamperfere with the twists and turns of the law. I wud surely be derelict if I wasn't to putt ye's right. D'er wis no seats the length and breadth of the train and derefore the young man has the crown given right to sit on yonder seat be it first class or no! If ye's wur tae ask me good an' humble self I wud have tae swear that the man in the winda' seat was the one who is wrong."

In response to this, Jimmy said with an opportunistic confidence, "Now there are seats in the other carriages I'll move into a second class seat."

"Well then off you go," said the policeman.

As the train pulled into the next station, Jimmy's smugness was abruptly displaced with the recognition that it was Johnstone. He just managed to get off the train as it pulled its way along the platform.

To his surprise, the man in the pinstriped suit and the policeman were standing on the platform and as Jimmy passed them, the policeman stood in his way and said, "Chust a moment, I want a wh'ord with you, laddy."

Jimmy defiantly snarled, "Aye whit is it?"

"What's yoor name?"

Whit dae ye want tae know fur?"

"Chust tell me yoor name," insisted the policeman.

"Wullie McGhee, wan-sivin-sivin Main Street, Rutherglen," replied Jimmy.

"What impudence," interjected the man.

"Whit dae ye mean; that is mah name."

"I wh'ould sincerely adfise you not to be so insolent, laddy," said the policeman.

"Look Ah'm gonny be late for mah work so tell me whit ye's want."

The policeman went on at considerable length, in his West Highland way which betrayed more the heart of a poet than the beat of a policeman, about how fortunate it was that Doctor Millar was not preferring charges.

During this, Jimmy kept repeating in his head, "bonkers bonkers away an' pull yer plonkers."

When the constable had finished Jimmy snapped, "Can ah go tae mah work noo?"

After crossing the footbridge, Jimmy stopped and shouted, "Mah name's no Wullie McGhee anyway, ya coupla diddies," and as he gestured a vigorous two fingered salute, he turned and ran into the ticket inspector. The inspector grabbed him by the sleeve of his duffle coat and as Jimmy struggled the coat came clean off him and he ran off up the road laughing.

"Ha ha, a square go wi' an empty coat, aye ye's'll no' get me noo."

When Jimmy got to the works gate, the security man smiled, "You've no' forgot ye'r identity pass again. Where've ye left it this time? Where's ye'r jaikit, anyway?"

Jimmy's face went white, he looked up to the sky and said, "Life's just a bowl a' effin cherries."

THE TWO SONGS that follow illustrate vividly the contrasting perspectives on life in Glasgow before the slum clearances at the close of World II. Nostalgia for that period is certainly strong among Glasgow people. This can be accounted for in many ways but primarily, I think, in the death of the communal spirit which followed the destruction of the old tenement communities. Life in the far-flung housing schemes took on a harrowing quality which the Council and its planners, in their zest to sweep the city clean of the unmanageable poor, lacked the imagination to foresee. Although McLean's song was written in opposition to McNaughton's, they are in fact complementary: each a truthful enough evocation of the period. If McNaughton's has a tenderer hue, this may be because he lays more stress on childhood experiences, whereas McLean's is more redolent of the grown-up world. On its own, neither is the whole story, but there is a lot of good fun in each.

It ought to be mentioned that a bastardised version of McNaughton's lines seems to have gained some currency due to Prince Charles' inimitable rendering on the opening day of Glasgow's Garden Festival. 'Soady scones', needless to say, were seldom 'soddy'.

ADAM McNAUGHTON

The Glasgow I Used To Know

Oh where is the Glasgow where I used tae stey,
The white wally closes done up wi' pipe cley;
Where ye knew every neighbour frae first floor tae third,
And tae keep your door locked was considered absurd.
Do you know the folk staying next door tae you?

And where is the wee shop where I used tae buy
A quarter o' totties, a tupenny pie,
A bag o' broken biscuits an' three totty scones,
An' the wumman aye asked, "How's your maw getting on?"
Can your big supermarket give service like that?

And where is the wean that once played in the street,
Wi' a jorrie, a peerie, a gird wi' a cleek?
Can he still cadge a hudgie an' dreep aff a dyke,

Or is writing on walls noo the wan thing he likes?
Can he tell Chickie Mellie frae Hunch, Cuddy, Hunch?

And where is the tram-car that once did the ton
Up the Great Western Road on the old Yoker run?
The conductress aye knew how tae deal wi' a nyaff –
"If ye're gaun, then get oan, if ye're no, then get aff!"
Are they ony like her on the buses the day?

And where is the chip shop that I knew sae well,
The wee corner cafe where they used tae sell
Hot peas and brae an' MacCallums an' pokes
An' ye knew they were Tallies the minute they spoke:
"Dae ye want-a-da raspberry ower yer ice-cream?"

Oh where is the Glasgow that I used tae know,
Big Wullie, wee Shooey, the steamie, the Co.,
The shilpet wee bauchle, the glaiket big dreep,
The ba' on the slates, an' yer gas in a peep?
If ye scrape the veneer aff, are these things still there?

*   *   *

JIM McLEAN

Farewell to Glasgow

Where is the Glasgow I used to know?
The tenement buildings that let in the snow,
Through the cracks in the plaster the cold wind did blow.
And the water we washed in was fifty below.

We read by the gaslight, we had nae T.V.,
Hot porridge for breakfast, cold porridge for tea,

And some weans had rickets and some had T.B.,
Aye, that's what the Glasgow of old means to me.

Noo the neighbours complained if we played wi' a ba',
Or hunch-cuddy-hunch against somebody's wa',
If we played kick-the-can we'd tae watch for the law,
And the polis made sure we did sweet bugger a'.

And we huddled together to keep warm in bed,
We had nae sheets or blankets, just auld coats instead,
And a big balaclava to cover your head,
"And God, but it's cold" was the only prayer said.

Noo there's some say that tenement living was swell,
That's the wally-close toffs who had doors wi' a bell,
Two rooms and a kitchen and a bathroom as well,
While the rest of us lived in a single-end hell.

So wipe aff that smile when you talk o' the days,
Ye lived in the Gorbals or Cowcaddens ways,
Remember the rats and the mice ye once chased,
For tenement living was a bloody disgrace.

ALEXANDER RODGER
(1784-1846)

FEW CAN GROVEL like the coarse-grained Scottish gentry when there's English royalty about. When George IV came to have a look at his Scottish subjects in 1822, Sir Walter Scott was out there showing himself off with a nauseating display of buttering up called, 'Carle, Now the King's Come'. To show that the voice of the people, in the language of the people, will always sound the truest note, the Glasgow poet, Sandy Rodger, composed this magnificent send-up of Scott, 'Sawney, Now the King's Come', which, we are told, outraged Scott's sense of loyalty. Scott was, after all, stage managing George IV's coronation visit north – the first Prince of the House of Hanover to set foot in Scotland since 'the butcher Cumberland' ran amuck at Culloden. When Scott rowed out to the royal yacht anchored in the Roads of Leith, the King welcomed him on board, 'the man in Scotland I most wish to see', and drank the poet's health in a bumper of malt whiskey. Scott begged to be allowed to keep the 'precious vessel' that had touched the royal cake-hole. Being granted this boon, he tucked it away in his coat-tail pocket and, as you've no doubt guessed, it wasn't too long before the priceless crystal was just splinters in his arse. Although the author of 'Waverley' let out the most awful scream, as Lockhart informs us in his typically complacent way, 'the scar was of no great consequence'. But as a memorial to a King's toast on the quarter-deck of the Royal George, it was certainly something. The only pity is, Sandy Rodger didn't know about it. 'Sawney, Now the King's Come' might have had at least one extra sample of the ridiculousness of bourgeois Edinburgh in 1822.

Sawney, Now The King's Come

Written in 1822

Sawney, now, the king's come,
Sawney, now, the king's come,
Kneel, and kiss his gracious —,
Sawney, now, the king's come.

In Holyroodhouse lodge him snug,
And butter weel his sacred lug,
Wi' stuff wad a Frenchman ugg,
Sawney, now, the king's come.
     Sawney, &c.

Tell him he is great and good,
And come o' Scottish royal blood, –
To your hunkers – lick his fud, –
Sawney, now, the king's come.
     Sawney, &c.

Tell him he can do nae wrang,
That he's mighty, heigh, and strang,
That you and yours to him belang,
Sawney, now, the king's come.
     Sawney, &c.

Swear he's sober, chaste, and wise,
Praise his portly shape and size,
Roose his *whiskers* to the skies,
Sawney, now, the king's come.
     Sawney, &c.

Mak' your *lick-fud* bailie core,
Fa' down behint him – not before,
His great posteriors to adore,
Sawney, now, the king's come.
     Sawney, &c.

Mak' your tribe in good *black claith,*
Extol, till they rin short o' breath,
The great "DEFENDER O' THE FAITH,"
Sawney, now, the king's come.
     Sawney, &c.

Mak' your Peers o' high degree,
Crouching low on bended knee,
Great him wi' a "Wha wants me?"
Sawney, now, the king's come.
     Sawney, &c.

Mak' his glorious kingship dine
On good sheep-heads and haggis fine,
Hotchpotch, too, Scotch collops syne,
Sawney, now, the king's come.
      Sawney, &c.

And if there's in St James' Square,
Ony *thing* that's fat and fair,
Treat him nightly wi' sic ware,
Sawney, now, the king's come.
      Sawney, &c.

Shaw him a' your *biggings* braw,
Your castle, college, brigs, an' a',
Your jail, and royal *forty-twa,*
Sawney, now, the king's come.
      Sawney, &c.

And when he rides Auld Reekie through,
To bless you wi' a kingly view,
Charm him wi' your "Gardyloo,"
Sawney, now, the king's come.
      Sawney, &c.

JOHN TAYLOR CALDWELL

The Battle For The Green

THE SUMMER OF 1931 was a riotous season in Glasgow. There were demonstrations involving anything from forty-five thousand to one hundred thousand angry protesters, in scenes which Police Superintendent Sweeny of the Central Division described as "a disgrace to any civilised community". The focal point of these demonstrations was Glasgow Green. Much of the disturbances took place just outside the Green, in the space called Jocelyn Square, but traditionally and persistently called Jail Square by Glaswegians, because of the proximity of the High Court and its incarceratory facilities. To most of those who took part in these demonstrations the issues were unemployment, the Means Test, and the Right to Work, but these popular causes were developments from the original grievance, which was the right to hold public meetings in the Green without a permit from the Parks Department.

This traditional right had recently been taken away by a Labour Town Council.
The Glasgow Green lies in the heart of the City, on the north bank of the River Clyde. It is the oldest of the city's parks, and is rated more than a park. It owes its origin to the common lands of the Burgh. A historian of the Green, writing in 1894, notes a civic function of this Open Space:

> One of the old customs of the Green remains almost as vigorous as of old... From time immemorial it has been the custom for all classes of preachers and debaters to air their eloquence upon the masses who frequent the Green; and on the Saturday and Sunday afternoons numerous knots of people are to be found listening to discussions on all varieties of topics.[1]

Another writer of the eighteen-nineties declares:

> But there are other shows which have long characterised the space between the Court Houses and Nelson's Monument, and which still continue with unabated vigour. From time immemorial it has been classical ground to the east-end controvertionalists. There Orangemen and Romanists fought bloodless battles by the thousand... There the stupid Tory, and the lofty-souled socialist...annihilates with ease all shades of

orthodox political opinion. On the Green the atheist readily confutes the arguments of the earnest Salvation Army; while the total abstainer has it all his own way in preaching the mission of temperance... Let it not be thought that the whole matter is bubble and froth, the phenomenon represents a vast aggregate of serious purpose, if not of deep thought, and it forms a most efficient safety valve for blowing off social, political, and religious sentiments, which might otherwise attain explosive force.[2]

The records of Glasgow Green are among the oldest existing records of Glasgow. The earliest known document is the Notitia, or Inquest of David, attested before the judges in the year 1120. It contains the result of the inquiry made by the command of David, Prince of Cumbria or Strathclyde (afterwards David the First of Scotland) as to the lands which had formerly belonged to the Church of Saint Mungo, and which he proceeded to restore to the new bishop of Glasgow. The bishop's property probably included the present Broomielaw, the old Green, or Docal Green of Glasgow, from present-day Jamaica Street eastwards, and the present Jail Square.[3]

After the Reformation these lands became civic property administered by the City Council. They were used for the cutting of peat, the pasturing and slaughtering of cattle, the execution of malefactors and martyrs, and for playing, strolling and talking. In the People's Palace, centrepiece of the Green, there is a painting which shows a crowd around a Glasgow character of Victorian days, Old Malabar. A later hand has painted into the crowd a little Charlie Chaplin, familiar in his bowler hat, cane, and big boots.

On April 13, 1916 the Glasgow Corporation repealed a bye-law passed on April 25, 1896 for the regulation of the City Parks and Open Spaces, and replaced it with the controversial Bye-law 20, restricting the right of free assembly. It was this which led to the riotous scenes of the twenties and thirties; and it was this that Guy Aldred challenged in the Green, on the streets, and finally in the High Court. The Bye-law, passed in 1916, was not invoked until 1922, when a Labour Council was in office. It read:

> 20. No person shall, in any of the parks, sing, preach, lecture, or take part in any service, discussion, meeting, or demonstration, or hold any exhibition or public show, for any purpose whatsoever, or play any musical instrument, except with the written authority of the Corporation, or the Superintendent, and then only on such places as may be from time to time set aside by the Corporation or Superintendent, by Notice, for such purpose.

On July 30 1923 this Bye-law was amended to make an exception of the space outside the gates of the Green, known as Jail Square. This concession was a recognition of the traditional usage of the Square. Meetings were being cleared from the gates of all other parks. Aldred was contesting the right to speak outside Botanic Gardens. But he considered Glasgow Green as a special case because of its historical associations. On July 6th 1924 he addressed an Open Letter, in the columns of *The Commune,* to the Lord Provost, Magistrates, and Council of the City of Glasgow in respect of the right of unlicensed liberty of speech on Glasgow Green, "as secured by long tradition, and respected by the Common Law of Scotland..."

The letter read in part:

> Sirs and Citizens,
>
> Today I shall be one of seventy speakers participating in a quiet and orderly meeting, duly advertised, which will be held at 3pm at the monument, Glasgow Green...
>
> At the present moment Edward Rennie is serving a sentence of fifty days as an ordinary criminal in Barlinnie Prison for speaking in Glasgow Green without a permit. Peter Marshall, Peter McIntyre, John Ball,[4] are waiting arrest for not paying fines. Seventy cases are pending... Meantime, a Labour Government being in power – for the *offence of addressing a lawful meeting* Rennie is being treated as a criminal...
>
> These Bye-laws were passed in 1916. Were they advertised as required? If so, how comes it that neither police nor public regarded them as applying to the Green? So much is this the case that in 1921, Mr Adamson, the present Secretary of State for Scotland, spoke on Glasgow Green without a permit. During the following years Maxton, Kirkwood, and Robertson[5] all did so. I submit that it is contrary to law to lapse Bye-laws, and then capriciously reimpose them.
>
> But the Glasgow Parks Act of 1878 confers no power on you to prohibit meetings... Section 37, the very section under which you act, concludes with this provision: *Provided that such Bye-laws shall not be repugnant to the laws of Scotland.*
>
> ...I submit that Bye-laws which send men to prison as common criminals for exercising the lawful right of assembly on a highway – and Glasgow Green is a highway as well as an Open Space – are repugnant to the laws of Scotland...

This Meeting was held as advertised, and meetings were held for several weeks thereafter. At all of them names were taken and charges made. The speakers were either from the *Antiparliamentary Communist Federation* or from the Scottish Workers' Republican Party, which had been founded by John MacLean. *The Communist Party* sneered at the "anti-pantis", and the "Claymore Communists" –

reference to MacLean's attempt to form a *Scottish Communist Party*. In *The Worker* the free speech campaign was described as a "stunt, pure and simple", and the Green described as a "bedlam of racing tipsters, medicine men, religious fanatics and political oddities."[6]

At a meeting of the *Glasgow Parks Committee* a report was read from the Town Clerk's Office, detailing complaints from the *Magistrates' Committee*. This referred to the abuse of Jail Square by racing tipsters, and other undesirable persons who had, since the speaking ban had been lifted from the Square, crowded into the place, attracting a rowdy and troublesome element, making "the place like a fair". The Magistrates' Committee recommended that steps be taken to prevent the use of the Square by such persons. The motion was therefore put to the Parks Sub-committee that the proviso exempting the Square from the restrictions which applied to the Green should be repealed, and that therefore unlicensed speaking on the Square should be an offence. There was an opposing amendement that 'no Action' be taken on the Magistrates' Report.[7] The vote showed eleven for the motion and eight for the amendment.

Guy Aldred was spending much of his time in London where he was conducting a campaign for the right to sell socialist literature, and to take collections at meetings in Hyde Park. In the course of this activity he had a brush with the police because he said disrespectful things about God. On Sunday 15th 1925 he was arrested from the platform and charged with blasphemy and sedition. Considerable press publicity was given to the charges, and Aldred was featured as an outstanding blasphemer. He conducted his own defence at a trial which ended on March 10th, and was found not guilty on all counts, except a minor one for which a fine of £2 was imposed.

These and other activities kept him away from the Green, but when he heard that the Glasgow Corporation had made application to the Sheriff Principle A. O. M. Mackenzie for deletion of the clause in the Bye-law which exempted Jail Square from the restrictions which applied to the Green, he lodged notice of objection. The date of the Hearing was advanced a week and on March 29th 1925 Guy Aldred appeared in person to state his objections. The Corporation was represented by Mr R. J. Campbell of the Town Clerk's Office.

Aldred quoted Acts of Parliament and legal authorities to support his view that the Bye-law was repugnant to the laws of Scotland and *ultra vires* of the Corporation. It was a gross abuse of terms to place tipsters in the same class as public speakers. In London the authorities had extended certain laws which prevented tipsters from going into Hyde Park, but public meetings still went on. Glasgow Corporation had no right to close down the Green unless they were prepared to provide another meeting place. The Corporation's proposal was contrary to the good government of the city, for this act of regulation was in reality an act of prohibition.

He was interrupted while he was drawing a distinction between tipsters and public speakers by the Sheriff-Principle who remarked (amid laughter) – "You mean that free speech is more important than free tips."

Mr Campbell said that it was not within the contemplation of the Corporation that the repeal of the proviso would interfere with free speech as far as it was enjoyed in 1916. If a meeting was conducted in an orderly manner, and there was no suggestion that it would lead to disorder, or obstruction, in all probability permits would be granted to speakers.

The Sheriff: "The question is whether it is reasonable to cure an evil by depriving citizens of their power of free speech except with permits from the magistrates."

Mr Campbell said there was no complaint in 1916, and right up until 1923, or at the passing of any other Bye-laws. Sheriff Mackenzie took the matter to *avizandum*. On April 1st 1927 he confirmed the reverted Bye-law. Guy Aldred's statement was reported at length in the Glasgow Press, and on April 2nd *The Glasgow Herald* in a lengthy editorial approved the Sheriff's decision, concluding:[8]

> The Bye-law in question, however, only applies to parks, and it can be made applicable to this Jail Square pitch because it is technically part of Glasgow Green, which is a public park. Having established the principle that this area is to be subject to the control of the magistrates, we hope the Corporation may be stirred up to make use of such powers as they may have, or if they have them not, to take steps to get such powers as may be necessary to enable them to regulate street-corner oratory anywhere within the City.

The Reverend Richard Lee, then minister of Ross Street Unitarian Church, in the East End, and sometime Glasgow Labour Councillor, and active public figure in the city, wrote to the *Glasgow Evening News* for March 31st 1927 –

> It is lamentable that the citizens of Glasgow should treat so lightly the passing away of the freedom of Glasgow Green. How strange it is that the main defence of free speech should be left to a Sassenach, Mr Guy Aldred, who made such an impressive case on Tuesday from the point of view of ancient usage, legal right, and public interest!
> ...When Socrates laid down the foundations of the philosophy of rational research he had no official caucus to back him up. When Jesus established the principles of spiritual religion, he had no support from official ecclesiasticism. Today there is little hope from any body of hidebound ecclesiastics or politicians.
> This proposal of the authorities means the choking up of the foundations of rational liberty and social justice.

The *Daily Herald* for the same date carried the headline:

SILENT GLASGOW GREEN
All Meetings banned on Jail Square

The letter-press concluded:

> The ban on meetings takes immediate effect, so that tomorrow the
> Green will be silent, almost for the first time in many years.

And for several years it remained so. Then it was broken by the worn boots and
holy voices of the *Brotherhood of the Way* who arrived with wooden crosses and
evangelical zeal on the forbidden ground of secular dictate in the June of 1931. The
Brothers tramped through the United Kingdom – and were therefore known more
commonly as *The Tramp Preachers* – as they conceived Jesus to have tramped
through ancient Judea, preaching the Gospel of Brotherhood and Love. They lived
only on the collections gathered at their meetings, usually of the poor and
unemployed, and had – always in theory, sometimes in actuality – nowhere to lay
their heads. They were not much concerned about Caesar's Bye-laws. They were
arrested, lodged in police cells, brought before the magistrate, and fined £5 – two
weeks' wages. As they were persons of no fixed abode, no time was allowed to pay
the fine – which they didn't intend to pay anyway. They were therefore sent to
prison for thirty days in a city the motto of which was 'Let Glasgow Flourish by the
Preaching of the Word" – for doing just that.

John McGovern, I.L.P. Member for Shettleston, raised the matter in the House
of Commons. He asked the Secretary of State (W. Adams, Labour) if he would
release these men. Mr Adamson said he "would make enquiries" which meant he
would do nothing. McGovern pressed the point till "disgraceful scenes ensued"
according to the press. The *Daily Express* for July 3rd 1931, playing on the fact that
there had been a championship boxing match the previous evening, gave a witty
heading:

LAST NIGHT'S BIG FIGHT – IN THE HOUSE
Glasgow Member dragged out.

Space does not allow us to enjoy the full account, but we may have a snippet from
the heart of the story. McGovern refused to leave the Chamber as ordered by the
Speaker, and refused to go quietly when asked to do so by four stout, but elderly,
doorkeepers, in morning dress, with white shirt fronts and golden chains. So:

> One attendant took Mr McGovern's hands. Mr Becket, M.P.,
> pulled the hands off. Others arrived and seized Mr McGovern by
> the legs and shoulders. Messrs Becket and Kinley threw themselves
> on the attendants. Mr Maxton, sitting immediately behind, leaned
> forward, his long locks dangling over his face, and joined in.

...Slowly the struggling heap moved towards the door. As each successive pillar supporting the gallery was reached Mr Maxton was dislodged, but renewed his hold on the other side of the pillar. Mr Becket, seeing that his side was losing, took a leap on an attendant's back. Down they went in a heap on top of the others. Miss Jenny Lee, hardly a couple of yards away from the ring, shrank back a little. Messrs Brockway and Campbell Stephen (I.L.P.) played an unhappy part. They were neutral. They neither moved out of the way of the attendants, nor attempted to obstruct them...and were thoroughly ruffled by the wave which swept over them...

So the struggling mass reached the door and John McGovern was ejected, and was suspended for the remainder of the session. He had received nation-wide publicity and made it known to the press that he would speak on Glasgow Green without a permit. Guy Aldred and Harry McShane were among others who were taking up the matter of free meetings in the Green. A *Free Speech Council* had been set up and Guy Aldred, Harry McShane, Tom Pickering *(Tramp Preacher)* and Edward Rennie *(Scottish Workers' Republican Party)* had been fined (but not paid) £5.

Two days after his ejection from the House, Sunday 5th July, McGovern arrived at the Green where a crowd of six thousand had gathered. The police allowed the meeting to proceed, but took the names of the speakers. These were Aldred, McGovern, McShane, Pickering, John Heenan *(I.L.P.)*, Willie MacDougall *(Anti-parliamentary Communist Federation)*, Andrew Reilly *(Irish Workers' Party)* and Joseph McGlinchly *(Distributist)*. These made two Court appearances. Guy Aldred gave notice of appeal on behalf of all the accused, and asked for a Stated Case.

Harry McShane was a member of the Communist Party, but at this stage the Party was not involved in the protests. McShane had to "drag them in".[9] This is not surprising when it is remembered that Moscow did not think much of free speech, and would not have welcomed a Report in which the Party not only campaigned for free speech but did so in association with the bourgeois I.L.P., the anarchist Aldred, and the evangelical Tramp Preachers. But when the demonstrations began to spill over into protests against the high level of unemployment, and the introduction of the Means Test, the Party had to take an interest. But the national figures stayed away, leaving McShane to organise the Communist Party activity. His interest in free speech was genuine and he refused to soft-pedal it in conformity with Party policy. His work for the unemployed was equally serious. He was Secretary of the National Unemployed Workers' Movement and, later, Secretary of Glasgow C.P.

Aldred was not greatly interested in demands for the Right to Work. That wage slaves should demand burdens for their backs in no way matched his definition of socialism. The more youthful members of his group, the Antiparliamentary Communist Federation and of the group founded by John MacLean (then deceased), the Scottish Workers' Republican Party, used to answer the slogan shouters, crying *WE WANT WORK* with the counter-cry *WE WANT NOURISHMENT,* and to calls for a shilling more on Parish Relief they would add sardonically: *AND A BAG OF COAL AND WOOLLY DRAWERS!*

To meet this new dimension of the demonstrations the *Free Speech Committee* was turned into a permanent *Council of Action* at a meeting of two hundred delegates from several organisations held in Central Halls on Saturday September 19th 1931. The Council passed a resolution by the APCF delegate that the Council evolve the necessary machinery to cope with the "chronic economic condition which is the normal state of capitalist society"; and to promote the transfer of political power to representative Councils of Action.

It would be a naive historian who saw in this gathering of honest upright proletarians in revolt the beginnings of an age of brotherly love, the germination of a new society. The general atmosphere was of disharmony. Every Group hated and villified every other. Antagonisms abounded. Agreements were reached with ill natured reluctance, not in sympathetic understanding. Only the Tramp Preacher hated nobody (actively) in private; loved everybody in principle, and defied everybody in practice. In Court they raised high their wooden crosses, and bawled forth 'Onward Christian Soldiers', confounding the raucous-voiced ushers, and nonplussing the Stipendary Magistrate.

It was the confused motives and fragmented leadership that led to the riots of the First of October 1931. Aldred maintained that continued mass confrontation would get nowhere, except hospital or jail. He was in favour of meeting the Corporation on their own ground, in the Court of Law. They had violated a principle of the Laws of Scotland. He would prove it, and force the removal of the offending Bye-law. Then, with the right to meet in public assembly in the public parks, the people should use that right to meet in concourse and debate the next moves in the struggle against the system which bred unemployment and exploitation. McShane thought that Court action would meet with failure, and that no further advance could be made along that road.

McGovern, writing thirty years later, said that the Communists (i.e. McShane) wanted to take over the unemployed movement,[10] and that he (McGovern) wanted to prevent them from staging a riot. A laudable motive, but his method of doing so was curiously inconsistent. He and Harry McShane had, the very afternoon of the evening debate on the matter, addressed a meeting in North Hanover Street, at George Square, the municipal heart of the city, urging the audience to rally to the Green that evening. The previous evening McShane had led a procession of unemployed from Warwick Street, in the south side of the city, in the direction of the Green, but had stopped short of forbidden ground on Albert Bridge where, mounted on the parapet, he had urged his followers to gather on the Green the following evening, and to "bring your sticks". The crowd took up the cry.[11]

So on the first of October McGovern led the East End contigent of unemployed to Glasgow Green, where a hundred thousand persons were gathered (police estimate, 40,000). But there were no Communist Party leaders, because the police had sent word to the Party Headquarters earlier in the day that no marching to the Green would be allowed, but the Communists had not passed the information on to McGovern, hence his arrival with the East End demonstrators. The police sergeant later confirmed that such a warning had been conveyed, with the concession that the leaders could organise those who had unknowingly gathered on the Green into small companies and lead them away. Thus Harry McShane who had urged his followers to gather on the Green did not arrive there himself till it was (as he later described it) "pitch dark, and we couldn't see a thing".[12]

He, and his comrade, Bob McLellan, were getting a section of the crowd into marching order for the return journey, as suggested by the sergeant earlier in the day, when McGovern "appeared from nowhere" and put himself at the head of the demonstration – and that decided the police to act.[13] Police evidence at the trials which followed, said that there were "several thousand evilly disposed persons, armed with chisels, bottles, hammers and sticks, organised by the National Unemployed Workers' Movement – (McShane's adherents, as distinct from his communist comrades) and two hundred policemen".[14] McGovern was assaulted by the police and arrested at once. McShane found himself behind the charging police. He met a crowd which wanted to "have a go at the police". He told them they would be slaughtered, and led them through the Green, over the suspension bridge into the Gorbals and safety.[15]

McGovern later accused the Communist leaders of deliberately withholding the police information,[16] of not having arrived at the Green themselves, leaving it to McShane, who arrive only to run away.[17] The representative of the Comintern who was in Glasgow, monitoring the actions of the Communist Party, was not pleased. He sent for McShane and ordered him to go and get arrested "because McGovern had been arrested". In abject obedience, characteristic of the Communist Party leaders of the time, McShane was putting on his shoes to go out and get himself arrested, when the Representative heard that two policemen had been thrown over a bridge into the Clyde and killed. The Representative thought that under such circumstances it would be better if Harry did not get himself arrested but went to Moscow instead. Fortunately the rumour proved false, and Harry was allowed to stay at home.[18]

The rioting and general disturbance which had started on Jail Square on the Thursday continued over the weekend. The doctor who examined McGovern's bruised back in a police cell told him: "The city is in a grip of terror. The boys are smashing windows and stealing in every street. They are playing merry hell."

On the Monday Guy Aldred held a meeting in the Green, once more defying the authorities. He trounced both McGovern and McShane. They had stirred up the people, he said, for no other reason but to lead them, or to *seem* to lead them. There was doubt in the I.L.P.'s Selection Committee as to McGovern's suitability as parliamentary candidate at the forthcoming election. His behaviour in the House had embarrassed the Party. Now McGovern wanted to establish himself as a heroic public working-class champion, so that to replace him would be unwise. McShane was using this occasion to establish himself as the leader of the unemployed. There had been no logic in their actions, the purpose of which was blatant self-aggrandisement.

Harry McShane was at this meeting and heard Aldred's denunciation. He asked to mount the platform. He said to the great crowd assembled at this illegal gathering: "We have had the demonstration. A number of people are in hospital, a number of people have been arrested. The casualties are all on our side. Next time we will be better prepared."[19]

Aldred said that this was the kind of rabble-rousing he had condemned. Having induced a hundred thousand persons to assemble on the Green – when it was "almost pitch dark" neither McGovern or McShane had any idea what to do with them, or with themselves. A violent confrontation with the authorities may be desirable and necessary, and would most likely be a part of the ultimate confrontation, but this ill-timed violence was self-defeating. It only resulted in men being taken to hospital, or landing in jail. Several days later McShane was arrested.

It was not till January the following year, 1932, that McGovern, McShane, and ten others were brought before the Sheriff charged with assault, mobbing and rioting – McShane was excluded from the assault charge. Superintendent Sweeny of the Central Division confirmed that he had sent word to the Communist Party headquarters that a demonstration would not be allowed to march through the streets, but that persons gathering at the Green would be allowed to return home in separate processions.

McShane was acquitted, for evidently it had been his intention to conform to this arrangement. McGovern was acquitted because he had been in custody when the violence erupted. The ten others, rank and filers, who had "brought their sticks" were each sentenced to three months' imprisonment. There is no firm statement as to the number of demonstrators injured. Four policemen were hurt. Seventy-seven plate glass windows were smashed.[20]

Meantime Aldred continued with his own line of action. The Appeal by Stated Case against the convictions of Aldred, McGovern, McShane and others for speaking in the Green on July 5th 1931, came before the High Court of Justiciary on October 17th 1931.[21] The Appeal was unsuccessful, but observations made by the Lord Justice General in disposing of it were brought to the notice of the Parks Committee, and on March 3rd 1932 the offending Bye-law was repealed, and replaced with an amended Bye-law. This gave right of public speaking, literature sales, and collections on such places as would be set aside by Notice for that purpose.

Sheriff Principle Mackenzie confirmed this amendment of the Bye-law on June 8th 1932. He explained the difference in a note to his interlocuters:

...After the right of holding meetings in the portion of Glasgow
Green situated in Jail Square (even he did not call it by its official
name: Jocelyn Square) without a written permit, had been taken
away, largely attended protest meetings were held in the Green
without permits having been obtained and a number of
prosecutions followed. In one of these the accused, a Mr Guy
Aldred, after convictions, appealed to the High Court of
Justiciary. The case – Aldred v Langmuir – is reported in *The Scots
Law Times Reports* for 1931, at page 603. The Appeal was
unsuccessful, but certain observations made by the Lord Justice
General in disposing of it were brought to the notice of the Parks
Committee, and that Committee had these observations in view in
passing the Bye-law which I am now asked to confirm...

The existing Bye-law prohibits all preaching, lecturing, or
holding of meetings without leave of the Corporation, or Director
of Parks. The Bye-law proposed impliedly authorises the
Corporation to set aside by Notice places where preaching and
lecturing may proceed and meetings be held without permits being
first obtained. It seems to me that this provision constitutes a very
material distinction between the two Bye-laws."[22]

The part of the Green set aside for public meetings was known as the Old
Bandstand. The Council of Action accepted this arrangement, except for the
Communist Party. Evidently forgetting that the Party had not officially taken part
in the campaign, and had described the gatherings in the Green as a "bedlam of
tipsters and medicine men", they now said that *they* would have demanded the
"right to speak from Jail Square to Nelson's Column", which would have increased
the "bedlam of tipsters and medicine men", and curtailed the right of the young to
stroll, and the elderly to sit in the Green.

The Council of Action broke up. John Meenan went into the Town Council,
McGovern was re-elected to the Commons, McShane went, obediently and
reluctantly to Moscow. His heart was in Glasgow with the unemployed. Aldred
continued the struggle for free speech. He maintained that the amended Bye-law
applied to every city park, and that the Corporation was failing in its duty if it did
not set aside by Notice an area in every park where the citizens might freely meet
and freely discuss.

Now that the right to speak at a selected site in the Green had been established,
nobody wanted to do so. The new site – the Green itself – lay deserted once more.
The new attraction was the Hunger March. The Green was forgotten. Everybody
with daring and adventurous propensity and little else felt the urge to join the
threadbare horde on the great trek to London. Aldred went against the stream in
condemning this exploit. It was a ruse of the leaders to confirm their alleged
leadership, and advance their careers. They were *mis*-leading the workers. To
march to London was to acknowledge the authority of London. To stand and

shiver in rags before the House of Commons, begging for work, was to accept an
affirm their status as wage slaves. He wanted places to be set aside in the park
where the people could gather and discuss social problems and gather strength
defy their exploiters not, like the marchers, acknowledge them. But he was askin
too much common sense from common people. Banner-waving and slogan
shouting were more glamorous, so free speech was forgotten, and the Hunge
Marchers tramped their way into the mainstream of history, where their abjection
held in high regard.

NOTES

1. See *Glasgow Public Parks* (John Smith, 1894); by Duncan McLellan. (Mitchell Library

2. *Glasgow: Its Municipal Organisation and Administration* Sir John Ball, Universit
Publishers 1896. Woodside Library, Glasgow.

3. *The Council* ed. Guy A. Aldred. July/August, 1932.

4. Rennie, Marshall and McIntyre were members of the Scottish Workers' Republica
Party.

5. Guy Aldred, Rose Witcop and Margaret Sanger addressed a crowd of two thousand o
Birth Control in the Green in 1922.

6. *The Worker* Aug. 9 & 16 1924 and July 25 1925.

7. Minute of the Glasgow Corporation Sub-Committee on Parks, etc. 29th Oct. 1926.

8. Press reports, summarised in *The Council* July/August 1932.

9. *No Mean Fighter* by Harry McShane. Pluto Press 1978, p. 173.

10. *Neither Fear Nor Favour* John McGovern. Blandforth Press 1960, p. 73 & 75.

11. *Glasgow Evening Times* Jan. 18 1932. Guy Aldred's press cutting books in Mitche
Library give wide coverage of the Glasgow Green campaign.

12. *No Mean Fighter* p. 175.

13. ibid, p. 176.

14. *Glasgow Evening Times* Jan. 18 1932.

15. *No Mean Fighter* p. 176.

16. *Neither Fear Nor Favour* p. 73.

17. ibid, p. 75.

18. *No Mean Fighter* p. 176.

19. ibid, p. 176.

20. *Glasgow Evening Times* Jan. 18 1932.

21. Aldred stated objections to relevancy and competency of Complaint in respect that 1
Species facti libelled do not amount to a contravention of the Acts and Bye-laws libelled. 2
Written authority of the Corporation or the Director of Parks *ultra vires* and do not conforr
to the Statute. 3) Bye-laws, and amended Bye-laws repugnant to the Laws of Scotland. 4

Amended Bye-law not confirmed by the Sheriff of Lanarkshire. 5) Form of application and conditions of permit *ultra vires* of the Corporation. 6) No Bye-law exists specifying conditions under which persons may speak in Glasgow Green; and 7) Complaint involved questions of civil right which cannot be disposed of in a Court of Summary Jurisdiction.

22. Quoted from *The Council* July/August 1932.

SANDY HOBBS

Clyde Apprentices' Strikes

1912, 1937, 1941, 1952, 1960. In each of these years there was a major strike for workers' rights, based on the Clyde, which succeeded in seriously disrupting production in engineering and shipbuilding. Yet most of the strikers were not trade union members, and in most cases the unions gave the strikes only fragmentary, belated and rather reluctant support. The key to this seemingly mysterious side to the history of workers' Clydeside lies in one word: apprentice. The strikers were apprentices, organising themselves outside the structures of the trade unions, and in several cases winning important concessions from the employers.

Some people might say that apprentices are not 'real' workers, and indeed the employers found it convenient to regard them as 'learners' rather than 'workers'. Employers resisted the idea of apprentices being eligible for trade union membership or of trade unions negotiating on behalf of apprentices. They fell back on a traditional notion of apprenticeship as a contract between employer and parent. Some managements made direct approaches to parents to try to use them to force the strikers back to work. Yet their eagerness to pressurise the strikers into going back was due to the fact that apprentices had become an important part of the labour force. As modern production techniques gradually replaced the older craft skills, it became practically possible for apprentices to do many jobs just as well as time-served men. It was not lost on the management that it was in their interests that this should happen as much as possible, since the apprentices were paid much less than the skilled adult workers. Had the employers not taken on apprentices in such large numbers and had these apprentices not been given such an important part to play in production, there would never have been strikes on such a large scale.

The dates given at the start refer only to some of the biggest of the strikes. There were many others but the strikes that took place in those years are worth looking at one by one.

The 1912 strike was set off by Lloyd George's National Insurance Act, but it would be wrong to call that the 'cause'. The basic problem was low wages. The prospect of having to pay six and a half old pence insurance out of apprentice pay that could be as low as four shillings simply heightened existing resentment. Unfortunately, whilst in some areas low pay was made the foremost issue, other strikers used the slogan 'Down with Lloyd George'. (In fact, apprentices could only apply for exemption from part of the contribution.) Earlier strikes had been on a restricted scale, but this time it spread over large areas of the country. Starting on 8th August in Dundee, Glasgow quickly followed and at its peak over 6,000 Scottish engineering apprentices were on strike.

Strike headquarters in Glasgow were set up at the offices of the Municipal Employees Association, a sign of the official engineering unions' lack of enthusiasm for the apprentices' action. Local organisation seems to have been good, but the strike was poorly coordinated nationally. Strikers at John Brown's, Clydebank, went back after ten days but most of Glasgow stayed out until the end of the month. Some North of England centres held out a further couple of weeks. In the end, however, the strike ended with little concrete achieved. Only a few firms deviated from the Employers' Federation line and increased wages. The employers, made nervous by the display of industrial strength, wrote tougher anti-strike conditions into apprentices' contracts. Writing of the strike, Bill Knox does not see it as a complete defeat, however. Not only did it make official trade unions take more notice of apprentices' problems. It also showed that the apprentices had 'a hidden capacity for organisation and self-discipline which augured well for the future'.

In 1937, industrial workers were gradually improving their pay and conditions after the depression of the 1920s and early 1930s. Rearmament led to engineering workers negotiating higher wages, but apprentices did not benefit and this grievance brought them out on strike. Starting in late March, it lasted five weeks, with 32,000 out at its peak, 12,00 of them on the Clyde. Pay demands were soon broadened out into a campaign for an Apprentices' Charter covering training and trade union negotiating rights too. There was a wave of 'Youth Strikes' on the Clyde, including walkouts by non-apprentice female staff at Beattie's Biscuits and Barr and Stroud. Initial hostility by the unions later gave way to support and some adult workers came out in token sympathy strikes. Victory was not complete, but as well as pay rises apprentices were granted fixed proportions of any future increases in adult rates. Non-indentured apprentices also won the right to have union officials negotiate on their behalf.

In some ways, the 1941 strike was the most dramatic one of all. Not only did it coincide with the notorious Clydebank blitz, but it was the biggest dispute to affect the munitions industry in the whole of the Second World War. (This was partly due to the fact that it had the support of the Communist Party which soon afterwards changed its attitude to strikes because Russia entered the war as Britain's ally.) It is difficult now to picture working conditions in the engineering industry at that time. Despite the war effort, there was little conciliatory in employers' treatment of workers. (Churchill had to write to John Brown's to try to persuade them to open a canteen for their workers.) The strike was short and the special circumstances of the war led to a speedy Court of Inquiry. Apprentice representatives surprised many people by the way they conducted themselves and the Court's report was a vindication of many of the complaints the apprentices had made.

Victimisation by employers meant that the token strike action in 1952 snowballed into the next large-scale apprentice action. Clyde apprentices had organised a half-day strike on 7th February but when they returned to work next day some were suspended. When news of this spread, apprentices in many yards and factories came out in sympathy. The feeling generated led to a full scale strike in March with many thousands out in Scotland and England. On 21st March, the Glasgow Herald reported that 'Mr J. Reid' – Jimmy Reid – had successfully moved a resolution supporting the action at the engineers' National Youth Conference. On 1st April, an employers' spokesman was typically reported as saying that the strike was holding up pay talks. Ten days later, apprentice delegates accepted a pay offer roughly half of what they wanted 'under protest'. Once again only partial success had been achieved.

The last great apprentice strike was the biggest strike of 1960 and one of the biggest strikes of the decade. Officially, 347,000 man-days were lost. At one point 60,000 were out all over Britain. A Clyde Apprentices Committee laid the base for the strike with demonstrations and token walk-outs. The main strike began on 21st April, earlier than planned because once again some firms suspended people who had taken token strike action. The strike committees showed they had the will and the ability to organise mass action. There were collections and strike pay for the needy. 'Flying Squads' were went to contact apprentices in England and Ireland. National delegate conferences were held, From many quarters, employers, union officials and the press, came accusations of communist dominance, intimidation and general irresponsibility on the part of what they liked to call the 'Boy Strikers'. But the strike organisation survived until a national conference on 14th May called it off. The pay settlement that followed gave them less than they had aimed for, but once again apprentices had shown their industrial power and drawn attention to the 'Cheap Labour Racket'. There have been no more apprentice strikes of that size, and we can expect no more. Heavy engineering has declined, and with it both apprenticeship and the industrial strength of apprentices.

Some look back with nostalgia to these strikes, but do they have any great importance? We should not be surprised that capitalism used the cover of 'training' to exploit young workers. Nor is it surprising that some of these 'boys' had the political awareness and skills to run successful industrial action with little outside support. What is worth noticing, with regret, is that the need for these strikes is a sign of a weakness in the unions and in the working class generally. The unions failed to tackle the problems of cheap youth labour and did not capitalise on the apprentices' youthful militancy. We can criticise the union bureaucrats but they were not alone in this failure. Ordinary shopfloor workers often discouraged young men from even joining their union. "You'll have plenty of time for the union when your time is out." Luckily the young workers often ignored that advice.

NOTE: There are articles in the Scottish Labour History Society Journal on the 1912 strike (by W. Knox, No. 19, 1984) and on the 1937 strike (by Alan McKinlay, No. 20, 1985). Ian McKechnie and I have interviewed some of those who took part. My thanks to Ian for his part in our joint efforts to collect information.

RUTHERGLEN DRAMA GROUP

Caterpillar Talking Blues

*Eeni meeni miney mo your factory has gotta go paranoia in
Peoria...*

(Spoken to guitar accompaniment, roughly 16 bar blues in G.)

Well we're sittin over here in Illinoya,
We got a real good story for ya,
We're a multie national corporation,
Got factories in every nation.

All except one, and that's in Scotland, and that's in England.
At least ah thinks so.

See we looked at the economic factors
an we don' need that many tractors
so we threw a dart an guess where it landed?
Sorry boys, your factory's disbanded.

At least ah thinks so.
Sons of bitches are still in there.

Next time I looked at the situation,
them bastards had started an occupation,
just tryin to keep their jobs alive,
workin for nothin from nine to five.

Why that's next to communism
At last ah thinks so

S'what ma granpappy tol me, and he should know
He was Polish.

They sure showed their Commie link,
they built this tractor and painted it pink.
They said it was a symbol, but that was just a front,
they gave the damn thing to War on Want.

Me, I gave at the office. Or was that Bob Geldof?
He's a Russian too!
Geldoff, Smirnoff, Comiloff, Pissoff, Fuckoff,
It's all the same thing.

This thing was becomin' an awful drag
So we put an Ad in the local rag
Sayin', "You better toe the line now sonny,
Or you won't git no redundancy money –

An that would just break ma heart."

YeeeeeeHaaaahhh! Round 'em on up
And move 'em on out!

They might think they got us beat,
but we're OK in our hotel suite.
Wine and women and caviar,
unlimited drink at the hotel bar.

(Drunk) Sho occupy shhuh goddamm fact'ry
Who givshes a shit?

We offered them money but they wouldn't take it.
Now c'mon boys, you ain't gonna make it.
We got the power of international finance,
come on boys, you don't have a chance.

Just what have you got?
You got backing from whole trade union movement,
the support of the whole nation,
international solidarity with workers in Belgium and Holland,
this song from the Rutherglen Centre for the Unemployed Writer's Group
...............Shee-it! Let's get out of here, boys, the
Goddamm pinkos are takin over.

Well, we wrote this song cos it's what we think.
Cos we like tractors that are painted pink.

There's a whole lot more we could've said,
we might even have painted the tractor red.

With brown polka dots,
pink fluffy dice hangin on the window,
curtains, maybe a CB
Ten four Caterpillar good buddy.
Anything we want – after all, it's our goddamn factory.

We had to add this here extra verse.
Things might be gettin better, might be gettin worse,
but I didn't put no cash in a tin
so a hundred guys could get back in.

All or nothin.
That's what you said in the speeches.
So Uddingston or Illinois, what's it gonna be?

(Sung) What's it gonna be?

Written by the Rutherglen Centre for the Unemployed Writers' Group, March 1987, last verse Mayday 1987, when offers where accepted for the factory by a consortium.

Mary Friel, Eric Brennan, Gerry Murphy, Aileen Andrew, Peter Arnott, Alan Morrison.

FREDDY ANDERSON

The Orra Man

When Adam oot o' heaven
was hounded for his sin,
he knew not where on this wide earth
his labours to begin;
to leave him thus bewildered
was never in God's plan,
so He took a pickle wad o' dirt
and made the orra man.

O the orra man's a marvel,
the blessing o' mankind
he serves the needs o' ane and a'
in every race and clime.
O the orra man's essential
to fill and bile the can,
to sweep and brush and muck the byre
we need the orra man.

Your poor oul' maw is wearied oot,
she's never off her feet,
wi' making beds an' grub for all
she seldom gets a seat;
she cleans the shoes, she polishes,
she scours the pots and pans,
she'll tell you waht it's like to be
the poor old orra man.

Man launches into outer space,
and robots multiply
fantastic whigmaleerie gigs
now sail the starry sky;
wonders great we will create,
but try the best we can,
there's nae machine we'll make to match,
the good auld orra man.

When climbers conquered Everest,
they made that grand ascension
with sturdy will on hearts of oak
and an orra man called Tensing.
I'll praise the independent soul
yet show me him who can
sincerely say, he did it all,
without the orra man.

PHIL McPHEE

Hutchie E – A Monument to Corruption, Stupidity and Bad Planning

WHEN THE BULLDOZERS moved into the Hutchie E complex, situated in the Gorbals, they began to remove one of Glasgow's biggest eyesores. There were many who breathed sighs of relief that day, none more so than Pat Lally and his cronies, the Glasgow District Council, who were the architects and planners of a housing disaster of gigantic proportions. It was pathetic to read of and see pictures in the papers and on T.V. of councillors at the site of the demolition celebrating champagne-style the removal of the evidence of their crass stupidity and greed. A friend remarked at the time: "It's a pity the buggers weren't inside the buildings." That was a sentiment I echoed wholeheartedly.

Of the need for an extensive programme of council housing there can be no doubt. Many of the original inhabitants of the Gorbals (mostly Irish Catholics or descendants) had been herded into the large housing schemes like Castlemilk and Toryglen which were no better than huge open prisons with neither shopping nor transport facilities, so it was not surprising when there was angry clamouring for a return to their roots in the Gorbals area from large sections of the community in Castlemilk. Evidence of this is clear when you compare the population of Castlemilk today, approximately 24,000, to the figure of around 40,000 when at its peak. To ease the political pressures arising from the demands of large sections of the scheme communities to be rehoused back into their former areas, the Hutchie E project was dreamt up by the City Fathers.

When we examine what happened next it is not surprising many people including myself suspected that certain underhand practices might have been involved.

The contract to build Hutchie E was given to a firm called Gilbert Ash, an offshoot of the multinational Bovis Group. Gilbert Ash held a virtual monopoly of the renovation contracts which were being undertaken in Glasgow during the seventies.

The site of Hutchie E was situated above old mine shafts which had been flooded for years. Disaster followed disaster during the construction. After work was halted by flooding (sometimes up to two feet of water on site). When the complex was completed and the decorators moved in they were faced with walls running with water and doors lying off straight lines and moss growing *inside* the buildings. A painter who worked on the job told me that as he put the wallpaper on it just fell off.

Scandalously, the public were not made aware of these problems. The fact that shifts of men worked overnight on the eve of the opening ceremony by the Queen to make ready the flat which she was to inspect. This was because all the wallpaper had fallen off the walls, which left the contractors panic-stricken.

It was then left for the incoming tenants to find out for themselves just what they had got themselves into. The joke of the day was: "Come and see my flat in Hutchie E. It has all mod cons – even hot and cold running water in the walls."

Councils officials and Gilbert Ash then disgracefully conspired to shift any blame for their incompetence onto the tenants themselves. Ludicrous excuses were made such as: the tenants' heavy breathing, gas heating, sleeping with windows opens, condensation. All complete rubbish. These officials knew what the problems were and kept it secret.

The pressure grew too great for the Council to bear and they caved into the demands for repair work. Incredibly the contract for repair work was given to Gilbert Ash, the very people who created the problem. The mind boggled at the effrontery of all this. All attempts at repair work ended in failure and from that failure grew even more organised forms of protest.

The Laurieston Information Centre was the base of this organised protest and from there a campaign was launched which resulted in the rehousing of all 2,000-odd tenants. The Council then left the buildings to rot. With the dismantling of the complex Pat Lally and his cronies in the City Chambers are burying their past misdemeanours and mistakes but no-one who showed any concern for what happened will ever forget that for over twelve years Hutchie E complex stood as a monument to corruption, stupidity and bad planning.

*   *   *

Jimmy Sez

Glasgow smiles better than
the wee lassie
that tells me ma giro's
in the post

Alex MacSporran

JOHN McGARRIGLE

Write nice things

last night
as I sat by my typewriter
a junkie
climbed in my window,
I was writing a poem
a very interesting little poem
about the birds, the bees,
and a flower that I'd seen
that day,
the junkie
battered my wife
stole all of our money
and when he left
took with him
my television set
and my hi fi unit,
this unfortunate little incident
rather disturbed me,
it really put me off writing
my little poem
about the birds, the bees,
and the flower that I'd seen
So, I wrote about
the wind whistling through the trees
instead.

Refuge

Cold,
wind swept
lonely
that's the braes
in winter,
beer cans
dirty books
condoms
litter
the paths
and yet
there's something,
that defies
this desecration
a sunset
unsurpassed
and when
the snow
comes
to hide
the sins
of man
you'll find
in this
winter wonderland
a refuge

JAMES MACFARLAN
(1832-1862)

JAMES MACFARLAN'S FATHER was bred a weaver in Glasgow but long before the poet's birth he had given up that calling to become a pedlar. The boy travelled with his father throughout the length and breadth of Scotland and, having no settled domicile for any length of time, got smitten with very little formal education. The muse, fortunately, can sustain itself quite adequately, and is often the healthier, out of reach of schools and schoolmasters. A surer stimulus was his mother whose songs and stories from deep in Scottish history and legend fired her son's creative fancy and gave him a hunger for poetry. By his early twenties there was scarce a poet writing in English whom he had not mastered. In 1854 he trekked all the way to London on foot to find a publisher but the book did not sell. His second volume, 'City Songs', met with a similar fate. For a time he was employed by the Glasgow Bulletin, writing legendary and other tales. He was a frequent contributor to Charles Dickens' periodical, 'Household Words'. This brought in too little, alas, to keep body and soul together. Half-starved, and alone, he died of TB in 1862 at the age of thirty, leaving us only some few sheaves of the great poetic harvest he might have won.

The Rhymer

I stood at the rich man's door,
　　Mid a tempest of musical din,
But the vagabond name that I bore
　　Could find me no footing within.
In a tremulous accent I spoke,
　　And craved him a pitiful boon,
But the voice of the suppliant broke
　　Like a jar on the reveler's tune.

O to be stab'd with scorn,
　　To bleed at a rich man's gate—
A rose-leaf cut by a thorn
　　And strewed by the breezes of hate.
With a word that can cruelly kill,

And the side-long sneer of an eye,
And the blood that has leapt like a rill,
Struck to ice by a freezing reply.

But a voice rose up from the stones,
From the heartless stones at my feet,
And I heard its long-echoing tones
Like an angel-flight over the street.
And it struck on the strings of my soul
As it bade me be fearless and free,
And I heard its wild cadences roll,
While it cried, "Thou are greater than he!"

I was mean as a weed on a moor.
Of wealth I had near a plack,
With the shadow of sadness before,
And want, like a wolf, at my back.
But storehouses bursting with gain,
And weltering vessels had he,
Wide acres of pastoral plain,
And isles that are hugged by the sea.

And still as I journey'd along,
The daisy looked up with a smile,
And the lark arose with a song
That haunted me many a mile.
And I walked in a rapture of soul
With the music that stirred in the tree,
For the burden that ended the whole,
Was still, "Thou are greater than he!"

PETER ARNOTT & PETER MULLAN

Beechgrove Garden Festival

(Alec and Dougal potter about with watering cans, trowels, etc. Centre stage, a floral sheet or cloth covers two more figures. Dougal looks up and addresses the audience.)

Dougal: Oh, Hullo!

Alec: *(also taking note of audience)* Hullo, there!

Dougal: Hullo and welcome tae the Beechgrove Garden Roadshow. And today, Alec and are in... Where the fuck are we, Alec?

Alec: Well, today we're in a verra big garden indeed, Dougal.

Dougal: Fuckin' enormous garden, Alec.

Alec: That's right, Dougal, because today we're at the Glasgow Garden Festival. And isn't it miraculous?

Dougal: Aye, aye. Whit's miraculous, Alec?

Alec: It's miraculous tae find a Garden Festival in a major industrial centre sicas Glasgow, Dougal?

Dougal: Aye. For example, Alec, vit's that over there?

Alec: Well, that's whit we cry a green belt, Dougal. Parkheid. And it's right next door tae that lovely red, white and blue display, Brigtonus Masonicus, with that provocative wee splash of UDA over in the corner, look.

Dougal: Lovely, but for me Alec, this is where it all began, here at Queen's Dock in Govan.

Alec: Aye, well you know what they say, Dougal – flowers are a lot prettier than cranes.

Dougal: Aye, and the great thing about flowers, of course, is that they keep coming back, year after year. But once the cranes and the ships and the jobs have gone, they never seem to come back, do they?

Alec: Verra true, but I've got a wee surprise for ye here tae cheer us all up.

Dougal: Vit's that, Alec?

Alec: Well *(Alec whips the sheet off the 'display', which consists of a yuppy in a bowler hat, with a briefcase and tennis raquet clutched nervously to his person, and a suspicious worker),* it's this wee growth of Bourgie Obnoxicus, right here in Govan.

Dougal: Lovely.

Alec: Oh, he doesnae look too happy, Dougal, I'm afraid.

Dougal: We'd better get right down tae work here, Alec, it looks like.

Alec: Aye. On ye go then. *(Alec explains while Dougal pokes at the plants).* Ye see, the thing aboot yer 'Wee Yuppy', as we gardeners affectionately cry him, is that they're a fragile, delicate sort o' plantie. They're never completely happy until they're entirely surrounded by plants exactly like themselves.

Dougal: So, in order for your 'Wee Yuppy' tae flourish in a new area like Govan, we've got tae get rid of the hardier, not quite so nice 'Proletarian Skintibus', or 'Scum', as we gardeners call them. So, first of aw, we pull oot aw the weeds *(removes his fag)*, then *(watering him from can)*, we let the watter seep intae the living areas, and when they call the cooncil tae dry them oot *(drags him to far side of stage)* we repot them way, way over here in this dry, arid, desert region we gardeners cry Drumchapel.

(Yuppy, now with more room, gets happier, plays tennis, mixes cocktails, etc)

And if he tries tae come back, he'll find the area has been completely overrun by yer Bourgie Obnoxicus. This is the process known tae us as Barretting.

Alec: And tae the District Council, the area has been Laffertied.

Dougal: Or fucked up completely.

Alec: So here's yer new Glasgow. All the Scum chucked out on tae the Compost Schemes, and lots of pretty flowers and obnoxious yuppies, everywhere ye look.

Dougal: Remember, Alec, how in the old days we had tae wait for the scum tae work themsels tae death before we could get rid of them.

Alec: That's the wonders of the Scottish Development Agency for ye, Dougal. Cos ye know what they say?

Alec & Dougal: GLASGOW'S MILES BETTER...for yer wee yuppies.

(Yuppie whinnies in agreement, and the worker looks on.)

– END –

Performed by Red Heads: Kate Donnely, Libby MacArthur, Peter Mullan, Peter Arnott.

Find enclosed your free starter pack and cardboard cut-out

THE DRUMCHAPEL STARTER PACK

1. One fully trained Alsation dog, guaranteed to bite the neighbours weans, bark all night, crap and urinate up everybodies close but yours

2. One District Council Housing Department missive entitling you to a rent free flat in balmy Broadholm complete with hot and cold running walls and optional green slime.

3. One Navy Blue Snorkel fitted with baggy pockets holes underneath the armpits, and artificial rabbit skin hood.
(just the thing to keep you warm as you wait two hours outside the Post Office to cash your Giro)

4. One UB40 dole card, giving you unlimited half price access to swimming, golf and the theatre.
(American Express eat your heart out)
   that'll do nicely.

JOIN THE EVER GROWING IN CROWD WHO START AT THE BOTTOM AND WORK THEIR WAY DOWN

For further details please apply to your local D.H.S.S., Housing Management and Y.T.S. office.

From 'Not the Drumchapel News'.

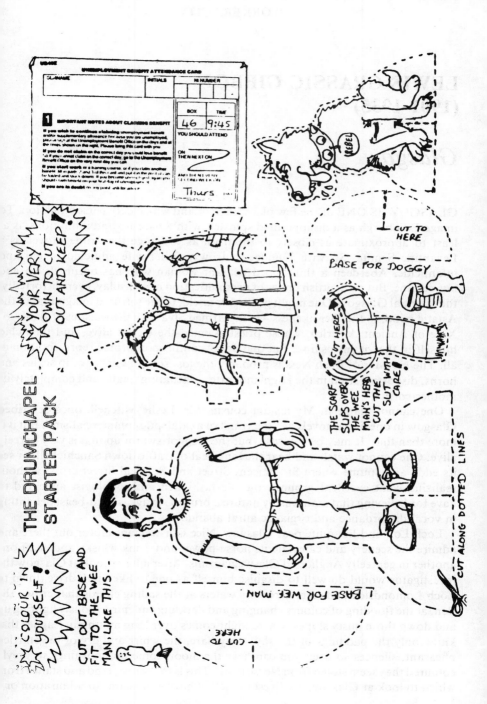

LEWIS GRASSIC GIBBON
(1901-1935)

Glasgow

GLASGOW IS ONE of the few places in Scotland which defy personification. T
image Edinburgh as a disappointed spinster, with a hare-lip and inhibitions, is a
least to approximate as closely to the truth as to image the Prime Mover as
Levantine Semite. So with Dundee, a frowsy fisher-wife addicted to gin an
infanticide, Aberdeen a thin-lipped peasant woman who has borne eleven an
buried nine. But no Scottish image of personification may display, even distortedly
the essential Glasgow. One might go further afield, to the tortured imaginings of th
Asiatic mind, to find her likeness – many-armed Siva with the waistlet of skulls, o
Xipe of Ancient America, whose priest skinned the victim alive, and then cla
himself in the victim's skin... But one doubts anthropomorphic representation a
all. The monster of Loch Ness is probably the lost soul of Glasgow, in scales an
horns, disporting itself in the Highlands after evacuating finally and completely it
mother-corpse.

One cannot blame it. My distant cousin, Mr. Leslie Mitchell, once describe
Glasgow in one of his novels as "the vomit of a cataleptic commercialism". But it i
more than that. It may be a corpse, but the maggot-swarm upon it is very fiercel
alive. One cannot watch and hear the long beat of traffic down Sauchiehall, or se
its eddy and spume where St. Vincent Street and Renfield Street cross, withou
realizing what excellent grounds the old-fashioned anthropologist appeared t
have for believing that man was by nature a brutish savage, a herd-beast delightin
in vocal discordance and orgiastic aural abandon.

Loch Lomond lies quite near Glasgow. Nice Glaswegians motor out there an
admire the scenery and calculate its horse-power and drink whisky and chaff on
another in genteelly Anglicized Glaswegianisms. After a hasty look at Glasgow th
investigator would do well to disguise himself as one of like kind, drive down t
Loch Lomondside and stare across its waters at the sailing clouds that crown th
Ben, at the flooding of colours changing and darkling and miraculously lighting u
and down those misty slopes, where night comes over long mountain leagues tha
know only the paddings of the shy, stray hare, the whirr and cry of the startle
pheasant, silences so deep you can hear the moon come up, mornings so greyl
coloured they seem stolen from Norse myth. This is the proper land and stance fro
which to look at Glasgow, to divest oneself of horror or shame or admiration or

very real – fear, and ask: Why? Why did men ever allow themselves to become enslaved to a thing so obscene and so foul when there was *this* awaiting them here – hills and the splendours of freedom and silence, the clean splendours of hunger and woe and dread in the winds and rains and famine-times of the earth, hunting and love and the call of the moon? Nothing endured by the primitives who once roamed those hills – nothing of woe or terror – approximated in degree or kind to that life that festers in the courts and wynds and alleys of Camlachie, Govan, the Gorbals.

In Glasgow there are over a hundred and fifty thousand human beings living in such conditions as the most bitterly pressed primitive in Tierra del Fuego never visioned. They live five or six to the single room... And at this point, sitting and staring at Ben Lomond, it requires a vivid mental jerk to realize the quality of that room. It is not a room in a large and airy building; it is not a single-roomed hut on the verge of a hill; it is not a cave driven into free rock, in the sound of the sea-birds, as that old Azilian cave in Argyll: it is a room that is part of some great sloven of tenement – the tenement itself in a line or grouping with hundreds of its fellows, its windows grimed with the unceasing wash and drift of coal-dust, its stairs narrow and befouled and steep, its evening breath like that which might issue from the mouth of a lung-diseased beast. The hundred and fifty thousand eat and sleep and copulate and conceive and crawl into childhood in those waste jungles of stench and disease and hopelessness, sub-humans as definitely as the Morlocks of Wells – and without even the consolation of feeding on their oppressors' flesh.

A hundred and fifty thousand...and all very like you or me or my investigator sitting appalled on the banks of Loch Lomond (where he and his true love will never meet again). And they live on food of the quality of offal, ill-cooked, ill-eaten with speedily-diseased teeth for the tending of which they can afford no fees; they work – if they have work – in factories or foundries or the roaring reek of the Docks toilsome and dreary and unimaginative hours – hour on hour, day on day, frittering away the tissues of their bodies and the spirit-stuff of their souls; they are workless – great numbers of them – doomed to long days of staring vacuity, of shoelessness, of shivering hidings in this and that mean runway when the landlords' agents come, of mean and desperate beggings at Labour Exchanges and Public Assistance Committees; their voices are the voices of men and women robbed of manhood and womanhood...

The investigator on Loch Lomondside shudders and turns to culture for comfort. He is, of course, a subscriber to *The Modern Scot,* where culture at three removes – castrated, disembowelled, and genteelly vulgarized – is served afresh each season; and has brought his copy with him. Mr. Adam Kennedy is serializing a novel, *The Mourners,* his technique a genteel objectivity. And one of his characters has stopped in Glasgow's Kelvingrove, and is savouring its essence:

"John's eyes savoured the spaciousness of the crescent, the formal curve of the unbroken line of house facades, the regimentation of the rows of chimney-pots, the full-length windows, the unnecessarily broad front steps, the feudal basements –

savoured all these in the shimmering heat of the day just as his nose had savoured the morning freshness. It was as good for him to walk round these old terraces as to visit a cathedral. He could imagine now and then that he had evoked for himself something of the atmosphere of the grand days of these streets. The world was surer of itself then, sure of the ultimate perfectability of man, sure of the ultimate mastery over the forces that surrounded him. And if Atlas no longer had the world firm on his shoulder, the world for all that rested on the same basis of the thus-and-thusness of things. With such a basis you could have the sureness of yourself to do things largely as had been done before. But the modern mind was no longer sure of itself even in a four-roomed bungalow. Its pride was the splitting of its personality into broods of impish devils that spent their time spying one on the other. It could never get properly outside itself, could never achieve the objectivity that was capable of such grandly deliberate planning as in these streets."

Glasgow speaks. The hundred and fifty thousands are answered. Glasgow has spoken.

This, indeed, is its attitude, not merely the pale whey of intellectualism peculiar to *The Modern Scot*. The bourgeois Glaswegian cultivates aesthetic objectivity as happier men cultivate beards or gardens. Pleasant folk of Kelvingrove point out that those hundred and fifty thousand – how well off they are! Free education, low rents, no rates, State relief – half of them, in fact, State pensioners. Besides, they enjoy life as they are – damn them, or they ought to. Always raising riots about their conditions. Not that they raise the riots themselves – it's the work of the communists – paid agitators from Moscow. But they've long since lost all hold. Or they ought to have —

In those days of Nationalism, Douglasism, (that ingenious scheme for childbirth without pain and – even more intriguing – without a child), of Socialism, of Fascism, Glasgow, as no other place, moves me to a statement of faith. I have amused myself with many political creeds – the more egregious the creed the better. I like the thought of a Scots Republic with Scots Border Guards in saffron kilts – the thought of those kilts can awake me to joy in the middle of the night. I like the thought of Miss Wendy Wood leading a Scots Expeditionary Force down to Westminster to reclaim the Scone Stone: I would certainly march with that expedition myself in spite of the risk of dying of laughter by the way. I like the thought of a Scots Catholic kingdom with Mr. Compton Mackenzie Prime Minister to some disinterred Jacobite royalty, and all the Scots intellectuals settled out on the land on thirty-acre crofts, or sent to recolonize St. Kilda for the good of their souls and the nation (except the hundreds streaming over the Border in panic flight at sight of this Scotland of their dreams). I like the thought of the ancient Scots aristocracy revived and set in order by Mr. George Blake, that ephor of the people: Mr. Blake vetoing the Duke of Montrose is one of my dearest visions. I like the thoughts of the Scottish Fascists evicting all those of Irish blood from Scotland, and so leaving Albyn entirely deserted but for some half-dozen pro-Irish Picts like myself. I like the thought of a Scottish Socialist Republic under Mr. Maxton – preferably at war with royalist England, and Mr. Maxton summoning the Russian Red Army to his aid (the Red Army digging a secret tunnel from Archangel to Aberdeen). And I like the thought of Mr. R. M. Black and his mysterious Free Scots, that modern Mafia, assassinating the Bankers (which is what bankers are for)...

But I cannot play with those fantasies when I think of the hundred and fifty thousand in Glasgow. They are a something that stills the parlour chatter. I find I am by way of being an intellectual myself. I meet and talk with many people whose interests are art and letters and music, enthusiasm for this and that aspect of craft and architecture, men and women who have very warm and sincere beliefs indeed regarding the ancient culture of Scotland, people to whom Glasgow is the Hunterian Museum with its fine array of Roman coins, or the Galleries with their equally fine array of pictures. 'Culture' is the motif-word of the conservation: ancient Scots culture, future Scots culture, culture ad lib. and ad nauseam... The patter is as intimate on my tongue as on theirs. And relevant to the fate and being of those hundred and fifty thousand it is no more than the chatter and scratch of a band of apes, seated in a pit on a midden of corpses.

There is nothing in culture or art that is worth the life and elementary happiness of one of those thousands who rot in the Glasgow slums. There is nothing in science or religion. If it came (as it may come) to some fantastic choice between a free and independent Scotland, a centre of culture, a bright flame of artistic and scientific achievement, and providing elementary decencies of food and shelter to the submerged proletariat of Glasgow and Scotland, I at least would have no doubt as to which side of the battle I would range myself. For the cleansing of that horror, if cleanse it they could, I would welcome the English in suzerainty over Scotland till the end of time. I would welcome the end of Braid Scots and Gaelic, our culture, our history, our nationhood under the heels of a Chinese army of occupation if it could cleanse the Glasgow slums, give a surety of food and play – the elementary right of every human being – to those people of the abyss...

I realize (seated on the plump modernity of *The Modern Scot* by the side of my investigator out on Loch Lomondbank) how completely I am the complete Philistine. I have always liked the Philistines, a commendable and gracious and cleanly race. They built clean cities with wide, airy streets, they delighted in the singing of good, simple songs and hunting and lovemaking and the worshipping of relevant and comprehensible Gods. They were a light in the Ancient East and led simple and happy and carefree lives, with a splendour of trumpets now and again to stir them to amusing orgy... And above, in the hills, in Jerusalem, dwelt the Israelites, unwashed and unashamed, horrified at the clean anarchy which is the essence of life, oppressed by grisly fears of life and death and time, suborning simple human pleasures in living into an inane debating on justice and right, the Good Life, the Soul of Man, artistic canon, the First Cause, National Ethos, the mainsprings of conduct, aesthetic approach – and all the rest of the dirty little toys with which dirty little men in dirty little caves love to play, turning with a haughty shudder of repulsion from the cry of the wind and the beat of the sun on the hills outside... One of the greatest tragedies of the ancient world was the killing of Goliath by David – a ghoul-haunted little village squirt who sneaked up and murdered the Philistine while the latter (with a good breakfast below his belt) was admiring the sunrise.

The non-Philistines never admire sunrises. They never admire good breakfasts. Their ideal is the half-starved at sunset, whose actions and appearances they can record with a proper aesthetic detachment. One of the best-loved pictures of an earlier generation of Glasgow intellectuals was Josef Israel's *Frugal Meal* in the Glasgow Galleries. Even yet the modern will halt you to admire the chiaroscuro, the fine shades and attitudes. But you realize he is a liar. He is merely an inhibited little sadist, and his concentrated essence of enjoyment is the hunger and dirt and hopelessness of the two figures in question. He calls this a "robust acceptance of life".

Sometime, it is true, the non-Philistine of past days had a qualm of regret, a notion, a thin pale abortion of an idea that life in simplicity was life in essence. So he painted a man or a woman, nude only in the less shameful portions of his or her anatomy (egregious bushes were called in to hide the genital shames) and called it not *Walking* or *Running* or *Staring* or *Sleeping* or *Lusting* (as it generally was) but *Light* or *Realization* or *The Choir* or what not. A Millais in the Glasgow Galleries is an excellent example, which neither you nor my investigator may miss. It is the non-Philistine's wistful idea of (in capitals) Life in Simplicity – a decent young childe in a breech-clout about to play hoop-la with a forked stick. But instead of labelling this truthfully and obviously *Portrait of Shy-Making Intellectual Playing at Boy Scouts* it is called (of course) *The Forerunner*.

The bourgeois returns at evening these days to Kelvingrove, to Woodsidehill, to Hillhead and Dowanhill with heavy and doubting steps. The shipyards are still, with rusting cranes and unbefouled waters nearby, in Springburn the empty factories increase and multiply, there are dead windows and barred factory-gates in Bridgeton and Mile End. Commercialism has returned to its own vomit too often and too long still to find sustenance therein. Determinedly in Glasgow (as elsewhere) they call this condition "The Crisis", and, in the fashion of a Christian Scientist whose actual need is cascara, invoke Optimism for its cure. But here as nowhere else in the modern world of capitalism does the impartial investigator realize that the remedy lies neither in medicine nor massage, but in surgery... The doctors (he hears) are gathered for the Saturday-Sunday diagnoses on Glasgow Green; and betakes himself there accordingly.

But there (as elsewhere) the physicians disagree – multitudes of physicians, surrounded by anxious groups of the ailing patient's dependents. A brief round of the various physicians convinces the investigator of one thing: the unpopularity of surgery. The single surgeon orating is, of course, the Communist. His gathering is small. A larger following attends Mr. Guy Aldred, Non-Parliamentary Anarcho-communist, pledged to use neither knives nor pills, but invocation of the Gospels according to St. Bakunin. Orthodox Socialism, ruddy and plump, with the spoils from the latest Glasgow Corporation swindle in its pocket, the fee'd physician, popular and pawky, is fervent and optimistic. Pills? – Nonsense! Surgery? – Muscovite savagery! What is needed to remove the sprouting pustules from the fair face of commercialism is merely a light, non-greasy ointment (which will not stain the sheets). Near at hand stands the Fascist: the investigator, with a training which has hitherto led him to debar the Neanderthaler from the direct ancestral line of *Homo Sapiens,* stares at this ethnological note of interrogation. The Fascist diagnosis: Lack of blood. Remedy: Bleeding. A Nationalist holds forth near by. What the patient needs is not more food, fresh air, a decent room of his own and a decent soul of his own – No! What he needs is the air he ceased to breathe two hundred and fifty years ago – specially reclaimed and canned by the National Party of Scotland (and forwarded in plain vans)... A Separatist casts scorn on the Nationalist's case. What the patient requires is: Separation. Separation from England, from English speech, English manners, English food, English clothes, English culinary and English common sense. Then he will recover.

It is coming on dark, as they say in the Scotland that is not Glasgow. And out of the Gorbals arises again that foul breath as of a dying beast.

You turn from Glasgow Green with a determination to inspect this Gorbals on your own. It is incredibly un-Scottish. It is lovably and abominably and delightfully and hideously un-Scottish. It is not even a Scottish slum. Stout men in beards and ringlets and unseemly attire lounge and strut with pointed shoes: Ruth and Naomi go by with downcast Eastern faces, the Lascar rubs shoulder with the Syrian, Harry Lauder is a Baal unkeened to the midnight stars. In the air the stench is of a different quality to Govan's or Camlachie's – a better quality. It is not filth and futility and boredom unrelieved. It is haunted by an ancient ghost of goodness and grossness, sun-warmed and ripened under alien suns. It is the most saving slum in Glasgow, and the most abandoned. Emerging from it, the investigator suddenly realizes why he sought it in such haste from Glasgow Green: it was in order that he might assure himself there were really and actually other races on the earth apart from the Scots!

So long I have wanted to write what I am about to write – but hitherto I have lacked the excuse. Glasgow provides it... About Nationalism. About Small Nations. What a curse to the earth are small nations! Latvia, Lithuania, Poland, Finland, San Salvador, Luxembourg, Manchukuo, the Irish Free State. There are many more: there is an appalling number of disgusting little stretches of the globe claimed, occupied and infected by groupings of babbling little morons – babbling militant on the subjects (unendingly) of their *exclusive* cultures, their *exclusive* languages, their *national* souls, their *national* genius, their unique achievements in throat-cutting in this and that abominable little squabble in the past. Mangy little curs a-yap above their minute hoardings of shrivelled bones, they cease from their yelpings at the passers-by only in such intervals as they devote to their civil-war flea-hunts. Of all the accursed progeny of World War, surely the worst was this dwarf mongrel-litter. The South Irish of the middle class were never pleasant persons: since they obtained their Free State the belch of their pride in the accents of their unhygienic patois has given the unfortunate Irish Channel the seeming of a cess-pool. Having blamed their misfortunes on England for centuries, they achieved independence and promptly found themselves incapable of securing that independence by the obvious and necessary operation – social revolution. Instead: revival of Gaelic, bewildering an unhappy world with uncouth spellings and titles and postage-stamps; revival of the blood feud; revival of the decayed literary cultus which (like most products of the Kelt) was an abomination even while actually alive and but poor manure when it died... Or Finland – Communist-murdering Finland – ruled by German Generals and the Central European Foundries, boasting of its ragged population the return of its ancient literary culture like a senile octagenarian boasting the coming of second childhood... And we are bidden to go and do likewise:

"For we are not opposed to English influence only at those points where it expresses itself in political domination and financial and economic over-control, but we are (or ought to be) opposed to English influence at all points. Not only must English governmental control be overthrown, but the English language must go, and English methods of education, English fashions in dress, English models in the arts, English ideals, everything English. Everything English must go."

This is a Mr. Ludovic Grant, writing in *The Free Man.* Note what the Scot is bidden to give up: the English language, that lovely and flexible instrument, so akin to the darker Braid Scots which has been the Scotsman's tool of thought for a thousand years. English methods of education: which are derived from Germano-French-Italian models. English fashions in dress: invented in Paris-London-Edinburgh-Timbuktu-Calcutta-Chichen-Itza-New York. English models in the arts: nude models as well, no doubt – Scots models in future must sprout three pairs of airms and a navel in the likeness of a lion rampant. English ideals: decency, freedom, justice, ideals innate in the mind of man, as common to the Bantu as to the Kentishman – those also he must relinquish... It will profit Glasgow's hundred and fifty thousand slum-dwellers so much to know that they are being starved and brutalized by Labour Exchanges staffed exclusively by Gaelic-speaking, haggis-eating Scots in saffron kilts and tongued brogues, full of such typical Scottish ideals as those which kept men chained as slaves in the Fifeshire mines a century or so ago...

Glasgow's salvation, Scotland's salvation, the world's salvation lies in neither nationalism nor internationalism, those twin halves of an idiot whole. It lies in ultimate cosmopolitanism, the earth the City of God, the Brahmaputra and Easter Island as free and familiar to the man from Govan as the Molendinar and Bute. A time will come when the self-wrought, prideful differentiations of Scotsman, Englishman, Frenchman, Spaniard will seem as ludicrous as the infantile squabblings of the Heptarchians. A time will come when nationalism, with other cultural aberrations, will have passed from the human spirit, when Man, again free and unchained, has all the earth for his footstool, sings his epics in a language moulded from the best on earth, draws his heroes, his sunrises, his valleys and his mountains from all the crinkles of our lovely planet... And we are bidden to abandon this vision for the delights of an archaic ape-spite, a brosy barbarization!

I am a nationalist only in the sense that the sane Heptarchian was a Wessexman or a Mercian or what not: temporarily, opportunistically. I think the Braid Scots may yet give lovely lights and shadows not only to English but to the perfected speech of Cosmopolitan Man: so I cultivate it, for lack of that perfect speech that is yet to be. I think there's the chance that Scotland, especially in its Glasgow, in its bitter straitening of the economic struggle, may win to a freedom preparatory to, and in alignment with, that cosmopolitan freedom, long before England: so, a cosmopolitan opportunist, I am some kind of Nationalist. But I'd rather, any day, be an expatriate writing novels in Persian about the Cape of Good Hope than a member of a homogenous literary cultus (to quote once again the cant phrase of the day) prosing eternally on one plane –the insanitary reactions to death of a Kelvingrove bourgeois, or the owlish gawk (it would speedily have that seeming) of Ben Lomond through its clouds, like a walrus through a fluff of whiskers.

For this Scottish Siva herself, brandishing her many arms of smoke against the coming of the darkness, it is pleasant to remember at least one incident. On a raining night six hundred and fifty years ago a small band of men, selfless and desperate and coolly-led, tramped through the wynds to the assault of the English-garrisoned Bell o' the Brae (which is now the steep upper part of High Street). It was a venture unsupported by priest or patrician, the intellectual or bourgeois of those days. It succeeded: and it lighted a flame of liberty throughout Scotland.

Some day the surgeon-leaders of the hundred and fifty thousand may take that tale of Bell o' the Brae for their text.

FARQUHAR McLAY

Toast o' the Monger's Man

Puir Glesca, blitzt an skrucken, did ye say?
Weill, rax yuir hairns a wee, cast yuir mynd back
Ti whit we wur: this ugsome toun
The cancer growth sae-caad o Bolitho.
Ye mynd o that? That wuis nae canard, tho
He micht hae gien mair fling
Ti hoosin plans the cooncil huid in haun
Projects baith practical an veesionarie
(Bit Inglis whan they traik on fremit grun
Hae een fur naething guid, aa's plague or ruin).

Think o the citie thit bleezed up wi MacLean
Cryan fur daith ti the rule o gowd
An the glead o revolution owre the Clyde
Ti sweep awa poortith an government:
Aye we wur seick that day, aa us
Wi the guid o Glesca tapmaist in wir thocht,
The mercantile citie par excellence.
Yit we won back wir power at the last,
MacLean we buriet an the lave we bocht,
Fieres o the common man
Their traitorie suin dowsed aa thae fires.

An yon degenerate loun wha wrote a buik
Syne droont hissel in the Clyde bit nane too suin
Aa menner o iniquitie lat oot
O' brothels, shebeens, razor kings an sic
Ramskerie plunderins and brigancie
As braith is sweert ti lowse apo the lugs.
The rope, the cat an Captain Sillitoe
(Whan jyle wuis jyle an no a laucht-at hyse)
Cuplit wi cooncil plans ti extirpate
Aucht slums maist vengeable fur fechts an noise,

The Gorbals, Brigton, Calton, Gerscube Road,
Tounheid, Plantation, Govan, Anderston –
Puit peyd ti aa thae ploys.

        Sae daur ye ask
'Whaur's cheraikter? Whaur's grace o livin gane?'
My certie, how thae fashions brank and birl!
Is it models or single-ends ye'd hae?
When we huid cheraikter ti droon aa else
We stude condemnit afore aa the warl:
We wur the citie o dreefu sichts, the hain
O' aa perversitie an blicht. A fig
Fur aa yuir cheraikter an grace!
Greek Thompson, Rennie Macintosh – guidsakes!

The cooncil huid ane darg: ti claucht this toun
Fae thirldom ti its ain daurk hert.
We wur the super-ego o the place
A'n clouran o this toun wuis conscience wark:
Ti redd-oot menseless fowk wi fousome weys,
The scaichers, hawgaws, methylatit cryles,
Ti wash awa aa reek o scelartries.

Glesca guttit-oot an clean
The wheels o commerce rinnan swift an free
The towerin office block, the motorway
An aa the people herdit oot ti schemes
Haill riffraff populations shuntit aff
Ti ghettoes at the faur pereemeter,
That wuis wir plan – a citie
Wi the warkers oot o sicht.

Ye dinna like it? People coont, ye say?
Wheesht, man. Did we no train the dug ti bark?
Aince in five years he does his wee bit trick,
Gey pleased ti dae it, an never failed us yit.
The people dinna ettle efter mair
Nor breid an harlequins. The same auld sang
As yon MacLean hissel wuis suin ti learn:
They'll gang the length o the preeson gate
Bit stop deid there.

Sae clink yer gless wi mine!
We'll drink ti the fower inseperables:
Fur ane athoot the ithers canna thrive:
Capital an Parliament, the Law an Power.
Lang may they haud together, till the hope
O' revolution, bocht and taymit, dees
Forever in the hert o man.

skrucken: *shrunken*
hairns: *brains*
fremit: *foreign*
glead: *fire*
lave: *the rest, remainder*
syne: *afterwards*
sweert: *reluctant*
aucht: *eight*
dreefu: *dreadful*
darg: *task*
thirldom: *thraldom*
menseless: *low, uncultured*
scaichers: *spongers*
cryles: *low, deformed*
taymit: *tamed*

rax: *stretch*
ugsome: frightening
gowd: *gold*
poortith: *poverty*
fieres: *comrades*
ramskerie: *lustful*
hyse: *frolic*
brank: *prance*
hain: *haven*
claucht: *clutch*
clouran: *to beat, chastise*
fousome: *dirty*
hawgaws: *hawkers*
scelartries: *drink-related evils*
(of the poor)

Glasgow's Smiles

Dear Sir, I must advise you that
Your house is going to be knocked flat.

We're going to take you from your slum
And put you in the lovely Drum

Or Easterhouse or some other scheme
Where the rain falls hard and the wind blows keen.

Your little street is lean and scrawny,
The ringroad's legs are big and brawny

And it squelches as it goes –
The only question being, Whose toes?

All must fall to let it pass,
Kinnen Park, Anderston, Port Dundas.

Your meagre little street won't shine
When leviathan calls to dine.

When leviathan comes on wheels
He's sure to be set on bigger meals.

We hope you won't quarrel with what we're doing
And kick up all that hullaballooing;

The Gorbals and Cowcaddens went
Withoot a murmur of dissent.

But if you must, then, say your say:
You may petition us all day.

And if wiseacres say, What a futile lark!
Just point to the toilet in the park.

That heap of rubble by the gate
Was a public pissoir till of late,

And when you mounted your campaign
Did we regard it with disdain?

Bulldozers at a single blow
Lewd and libidinous laid low,

And certain folks were most astonished
To find their rendezvous demolished.

True, that was part of another plan,
An 'unattended toilets' ban

And purely a police decision
Before we saw your nice petition:

(A confidential memo, that,
Which some fool couldn't keep under his hat,

But what's democracy about
If you can't come clean once the secret's out?)

Nevertheless the cooncil's dream,
Auld Glesca guttit oot an clean

Wull make some rich an ithers famous
An segregate thae yins thit shame us.

(This hamely daub we thocht tae scryveit
Fur fear yer lugs were sairly deaveit

No tae say yer puir wee harnes
Wi Inglis bureaucratic terms,

As weel's tae show, jist like in law
Scots can ootbureaucrat them aa

an tho we clack an tho we glower
We're great idolaters o power.

Fur thae puir sowls thit urnae followin:
WE'RE GONNIE KICK THIS CITIE'S HOLE IN!)

There's glory and there's hygeine too

WORKERS CITY

When you put your toes in leviathan's stew:

Think if in time to come they'll say,
He moved his arse for the motorway!

Or, Nero got it right in one –
A town smells better when it's gone.

Langmuir an Algie Earns

Ye mind the Setterday mornins at the Central
Auld Langmuir on the bench, stipendiary,
Wig ayways hauf-wey doon his face
Waitin fur the ten thoosan breaches
O' the nicht afore, an me wan o thim
Pullt in shakin like a scarecraw, ten stitches
In ma heid, nae jaikit an wan shoe missin.
'Sae here's wir handsel,' Ah heard him sayin
Ahint his haun yon wey: he wis laughin.
'Noo you own up an gie us aa a break.
We've got ten thoosan breaches to attend tae,
Fower hunner thefts o leid fae Glesca roofs
No ti speak o loiterins wi intent.
Then aa these fellas batterin thir wives,
An thaem thit lift thein hauns to constables –
Like you. Ye hear ma speak. Nae lah-dee-dah
Hauf-byalt wally-close stuff here. Ah ken yuir freens –
Kemp an Swiftie an Candy an Pie
An that craw Russo. Ah ken yuir howfs –
The Sarrie Heid, Burnt Barns an the Clyde Vauts tae.
Jeez O! Yis wuld sook thon wine fae a shitty cloot
An think nane o it.'

       Ma hert lowpt up. These soonds
Wur music ti ma ears. Ah've won a watch,
Ah thought ti masel, it's Calton talks. 'Guilty!'
Ah shooted oot. 'Guilty, yuir honour,'
(Gie'm his place), 'Ah'm guilty, Sir.'

But eftir – in the dug box up in Bar
Anither thought went thru ma heid. Ye fule!
Six months wull be six fuckin months
Whitever wey they say it.

ETHEL MacDONALD (1909-1960)

Ethel, one of a family of nine, was born in Bellshill and came to live in Glasgow as a young teenager in the mid twenties. Soon after, she became a socialist and mixed for a time with the ILP. By about 1932 she made contact with Bakunin House and the anti-parliamentarians, including Guy Aldred, and from this time on she became more and more identified with Anarchist ideas in the revolutionary struggle. A gifted linguist, she went to Spain in 1936 accompanied by her friend and colleague Jenny Patrick. Whilst Jenny travelled on to help in Madrid, Ethel stayed to work with the Anarchists in Barcelona. She was there during the famous 'May Events' when the Republicans had their own civil war behind the lines – with the Communists determined to break the power of the CNT even if it meant losing the war against Franco. For several days Ethel took part in the street battles on the CNT/FAI barricades. Of her many broadcast speeches on Radio Barcelona, seven were published in the *Bellshill Speaker* in 1937. 'The Volunteer Ban', the speech chosen here, was published in *Regeneracion* the same year. Ethel's whereabouts were unknown for several months after her imprisonment by the Communists. On her release towards the end of 1937, six hundred wellwishers crowded into Queen Street station to cheer her return. The remainder of her life was likewise devoted to the libertarian struggle. She, along with Guy Aldred, Jenny Patrick and John Taylor Caldwell, founded the United Socialist Movement and worked from the Strickland Press in George Street, Glasgow, producing in all 25 volumes of their monthly paper *The Word*. On 1 December, 1960, Ethel died in Knightswood Hospital. She was only 51 years old. In view of the nature of the illness from which she suffered – multiple sclerosis – it was her wish that her body be donated to the University of Glasgow for medical research in the hope that other sufferers might benefit. It was typical of the quality of mind displayed by this woman throughout her life. An invaluable collection of papers, posters, leaflets, letters and other historical memorabilia was brought from Spain in 1937 and, through the Mitchell Library, bequeathed by Ethel to the people of Glasgow.

*   *   *

The Volunteer Ban

TOMORROW, SATURDAY, THE 20th of February, 1937, is the date fixed by the Sub-Committee of Non-Intervention, sitting in London, for the commencement of the ban on volunteers for Spain. Volunteers to Spain! From where have these volunteers come? Italy has sent, not volunteers, but conscripts. Germany landed in Spanish territory, not volunteers, but conscripts. The army of rebel Franco consists, not of volunteers, but of conscript Moors, conscript Germans, conscript Italians, all bent on making Spain a Fascist colony and Africa a Fascist hell, with the defeat and the retreat of democracy everywhere.

The situation today proves the truth of the words of St. Simon and of Proudhon that parliamentarianism is the road to militarism, that parliamentary democracy is impossible, and that mankind must accept industrial democracy, revolutionary syndicalism. But syndicalism and industrial democracy do not imply trades unionism which is the British idea of organisation and action. If mankind is not prepared to accept this, then the only other alternative is a retreat to barbarism and militarism. An insistence on parliamentary so-called democracy is merely playing with freedom and in effect, retreating to militarism. The progressive conquest of political power under capitalism is a snare and a delusion. The present situation in Germany illustrates this truth very clearly.

If parliamentary socialism had any worth whatever, this could never have taken place. Germany could have given the world the example that would have set alight the fires of world revolution. But Germany failed because of this paralysing belief in parliamentarianism and this disbelief in the power and initiative of the working class. It has been left to Spain, with its Anarcho-syndicalism, to do what Germany should have done. And this paralysis extends to other countries that still believe in the power of parliament as an emancipating weapon of the proletariat. It should act as such but that is beyond its power. Belief in parliament does not lead to freedom, but leads to the emancipation of a few selected persons at the expense of the whole of the working class.

What are the actions of the parliamentary parties with regard to support of the Spanish struggle? They talk, they discuss, they speak with bated breath of the horrors that are taking place in Spain. They gesticulate, they proclaim to the world their determination to assist Spain and to see that Fascism is halted; and that is all they do. Talk of what they will do. This would not matter if it were not for the fact that the workers, through a disbelief in their own power to do something definite, collaborate with them in this playing with words.

Comrades, fellow-workers, of what use are your meetings that pass pious resolutions, that exhibit Soldiers of the International Column, provide entertainment, make collections and achieve nothing? This is not the time for sympathy and charity. This is the time for action. Do you not understand that every week, every day and every hour counts. Each hour that passes means the death of more Spanish men and women, and yet you advertise meetings, talk, arrange to talk and fail to take any action. Your leaders ask questions in parliament, in the senate, collect in small committees and make arrangements to send clothes and food to the poor people of Spain who are menaced by this horrible monster of Fascism, and in the end, do nothing.

We welcome every man that comes to Spain to offer his life in the cause of freedom. But of what use are these volunteers if we have no arms to give them? We want arms, ammunition, aeroplanes, all kinds of war material. Your brothers who come to us to fight and have no arms to fight with are also being made a jest of by your inaction. We want the freedom of the Mediterranean. We want our rights, the rights that are being taken from us by the combined efforts of international capitalism. You have permitted Franco to have soldiers and arms and aeroplanes and ammunition. Your government, in the name of democracy, have starved the government and workers of Spain, and now they have decided to ban arms, ban volunteers, to the government of the Spanish workers. Your government, workers of the world, are assisting in the development of Fascism. They are conniving at the defeat of the workers' cause, and you tamely accept this or merely idly protest against it. Workers, your socialism and your communism are worthless. Your democracy is a sham, and that sham is fertilising the fields of Spain with the blood of the Spanish people. Your sham democracy is making the men, women and children of Spain the sod of Fascism. The workers of Spain bid you cry, "Halt!" The workers of Spain bid you act!

I, myself, was in Scotland when sanctions were proposed on behalf of Ethiopia. The Labour Party there threatened war. The Trades Unions threatened war. The Communist Party threatened war. The threats wore off, and Italy seized the land of Ethiopia, and despite the continued protests from various persons, Italy has commenced the exploitation of Abyssinia. Ethiopia is now the colony of Italy.

But Abyssinia is not Spain. Despite its history, Abyssinia is a wild and undeveloped country and may, indeed, in some parts, be semi-savage. But Spain is a land of culture and more important, a land of proletarian development, and it is menaced by the hireling Franco because it possesses proletarian culture. And Franco is assisted by Hitler and Mussolini and all the hordes of international capitalism because of the wealth contained within its territory, and to gain possession of that wealth for purposes of further exploiting the working class and for their own personal aggrandisement, they are prepared to massacre the whole of the Spanish working class. For what are the lives of the workers to them? Labour is cheap, and is easily replaceable.

And you, parliamentarians, you so-called socialists, talk and talk, and know not how to act. Nor when to act. For Spain, you are not even prepared to threaten war. Non-intervention, as a slogan, is an improvement on sanctions. It is even more radically hypocritical. It is more thorough and deliberate lying, for Non-intervention means the connived advance of Fascism. This cannot be disputed. Under the cloak of Non-intervention, Hitler and Mussolini are being assisted in their wanton destruction of Spain. Non-intervention gives them the excuse to do nothing, and behind the scenes to supply these European maniacs with all that they require. Your governments are not for non-intervention. They stand quite definitely for intervention, intervention on behalf of their friends and allies, Hitler and Mussolini. Your governments and your leaders have many points in common with these two scoundrels. All of them lack decency, human understanding, and intelligence. They are virtually the scum of the earth, the dregs that must be destroyed.

Comrades, workers, Malaga has fallen. Malaga was betrayed and you too were betrayed, for you have witnessed not merely the fall of Malaga but the fall of a key defence of world democracy, of workers' struggle, of world liberty, of world emancipation. Malaga fell; you, the world proletariat, were invaded: and you talk. Talk and lament and sigh and fear to act! Tomorrow, Madrid may be bombed once more. Barcelona may be attacked. Valencia may be attacked, and still you talk! When will this talking cease? Will you never act?

To go back to Germany. At the Second Congress of the Third International, Moscow, a comrade who is with us now in Spain, answering Zinoviev, urged faith in the syndicalist movement in Germany and the end of parliamentary communism. He was ridiculed. Parliamentarianism, communist parliamentarianism, but still parliamentarianism would save Germany. And it did. You know this. You know the conditions in that famous land today. Yes, parliamentarianism saved Germany. Saved it from Socialism. Saved it for Fascism. Parliamentary social democracy and parliamentary communism have destroyed the socialist hope of Europe, has made a carnage of human liberty. In Britain, parliamentarianism saved the workers from Socialism, gave them a Socialist leader of a National Government, and has prepared the workers for the holocaust of a new war. All this has parliamentarianism done. Have you not had enough of this huge deception? Are you still prepared to continue in the same old way, along the same old lines, talking and talking and doing nothing?

Spain, syndicalist Spain, the Spanish workers' republic would save you. Yes, save you with the hunger and blood and struggle of its magnificent people. And you pause and hesitate to gave your solidarity, and pause in your manhood and democracy of action until it is too late.

The crisis is here. The hour of struggle is here. Now is the decisive moment. By all your traditions of liberty and struggle, by all the brave martyrs of old, in the name of the heroic Spanish men and women, I bid you act. Act on behalf of

Spain through living, immediate Committees of Action in Britain, in America, throughout the whole world. Let your cry be not non-intervention, but "Hands off Spain", and from that slogan let your action come. In your trade union branches, in your political party hall, make that your cry: "All Hands off Spain". What will your action be? The General Strike. Your message? "Starve Fascism, end the war on Spanish Labour, or – the Strike, the strike and on to Revolution".

The British Government says: "You shall not serve in Spain." Good! Then to the British Workers we say make this your reply. "We will serve Spain and the workers in Spain and ourselves in Britain. We strike." Down tools! There is one flag of labour today. Spain's Red and Black Flag of Freedom, of Syndicalism and Courage!

"Workers of the world! Rally! Think – and act now!"

ROBERT LYNN

Not a Life Story, Just a Leaf From It

> The State is a condition, a certain relationship between human
> beings, a mode of human behaviour: we destroy it by
> contracting other relationships, by behaving differently... One
> day it will be realised that Socialism is not the invention of
> anything new but the discovery of something that was always
> present, of something that has grown.
>
> *Gustav Landauer*

WHEN I WAS an apprentice engineer in Yarrow's I was already reading Marx.
At the time I started my apprenticeship I was very naive. The Catholic Church
and State indoctrination ha√l done their usual mischief. But industry freed me
from all that and it didn't take too long. Industry became my university. There
was a good class-conscious and political education running alongside my
engineering training. Whilst serving my time I had the good fortune to encounter
some engineers and other grades of workers who were quite erudite. These
people read important books and argued about what they read. There was
always some social or political or philosophical controversy going on. Listening
to these, and indeed taking part in them as far as I was able at the time, soon
annihilated my shallow metaphysical religiosity. I began to question everything
and examine things for myself and the scientific analysis of religion led on to the
scientific analysis of the economic and political system. It was a logical step. If
the first was a fraud, the other might be as well. I was introduced to a lot of
literature on economics, mostly short popular works and pamphlets. I soon grew
dissatisfied with these because they kept referring back and taking their
authority from major works in the past. I decided to go in at the deep end and
take on the major works for myself. That's how I started reading Marx. It was a
long hard slog but well worth it. I had to acquire a whole new vocabulary. But if
you have to struggle a bit at the outset, things usually take better hold in the
understanding. It's better than just making do with other people's commentaries
and second-hand interpretations.

I was certainly drawn to Communism but not the Communist Party. There
were many ex-Catholics in the CP at that time. I knew plenty of them. It was I
suppose a kind of home from home for a lot of them. It had the same kind of rigid

hierarchical structure after all, with a few people at the top doing all the thinking, making all the decisions and keeping all the control. I saw through that all right. Perhaps I should say I was drawn to Socialism. But the terms Communism and Socialism are really interchangeable. It was Lenin who falsely differentiated between them.

When Lenin was advocating State Capitalism in Russia he claimed that this was 'Socialism' which would, in time, with the development of production and technology, finally transform into 'true red-blooded Communism'. This was just doubletalk. And if you became a member of the CP you went about parroting this doubletalk. This was what they called Party discipline. I suppose it was my resistance to this kind of discipline which kept me out of the CP. Probably at that time it was more a matter of temperament than anything else. But then came the Apprentices' Strike, which the Communist Party opposed, and that was enough for me. This was during the last year of my apprenticeship, round about 1943-44. I was on the strike committee representing Yarrow's apprentices. The strike was against the Bevin Ballot Scheme. Ernest Bevin was the minister of labour and social services. He'd made the blunder of sending too many miners into the armed forces. To remedy this he came up with the idea of suspending some lads' apprenticeships so he could then conscript them into the coal mines. Patriotism fell on stony ground in this instance. The apprentices struck. It was the first major protest I was involved in and it was completely successful. In something like three weeks Bevin caved in. The Communist Party had opposed the strike because Russia was by that time into the war on the side of the allies. Their opposition alienated me and numerous other young people.

It was Eddie Shaw who introduced me to the Egoist philosophy of Max Stirner. The history of human progress seen as the history of rebellion and disobedience, with the individual debased by subservience to authority in its many forms and able to retain his/her dignity only through rebellion and disobedience. Eddie was a brilliant Anarchist orator who drew vast crowds to the meetings, whether indoors or in the open air. Another popular speaker was Jimmy Raeside. In the Central Halls and at various other venues throughout the city the Anarchist meetings were jam-packed. I might add that, during World War II and for several years thereafter, the Glasgow Anarchist Group was easily the most active and vociferous of all the Left groupings in this country. There were of course regional contacts with staunch comrades in other groups. We had platform speakers from Burnbank, Hamilton, Paisley, Edinburgh and Dundee. Over any single weekend there must have been a few thousand people attending Anarchist meetings. I first came across the Anarchists at an outdoor meeting in Brunswick Street, towards the end of my apprenticeship.

The group had about sixty active members at this time. Not everybody had an aptitude for platform speaking. One would feel like doing such and such but not another. One might write but be disinclined to speak in public but perhaps would do so on occasion. Naturally most members had a shot at everything. I remember, for example, old Tommy Layden (he was old relatively speaking within the group). Tommy loved to chalk the streets advertising the meetings; he took great pride in his print and nobody could do it better. He also tirelessly sold the literature. Old Tommy breathed Anarchism. He always remembered the Commie and Trotskyite thugs who had often resorted to violence when they caught him chalking on his own. But he always spoke of them as if they were more to be pitied than despised. He was a refined, pleasant man and deserves to be remembered.

There were several shop stewards in the group. Eddie Fenwick was the convenor in Hillington (you had to be in the union in a closed shop). Eddie, like most in the group, had a Syndicalist orientation. He was somewhat shy of the platform but more than made up for this on a personal man-to-man level in the workshop where he spread the Anarcho-Syndicalist case freely. We also had a lot of stewards in the heavy engineering and shipbuilding industries.

There was a small group in the Royal Ordinance Factory in Dalmuir who were most definitely Syndicalist in character. Although Jimmy Raeside and Frank Leech of the central Glasgow Anarchist Group spoke frequently at the Ordinance Factory gate, I'm certain this group had roots in Anarchism independent of this, for a lot of them were a good few years older than Leech and Raeside. I remember them coming to Brunswick Street to arrange for the production of a pamphlet called 'Equity'. It was powerfully and indubitantly Syndicalist.

Charlie Baird was the secretary of the Glasgow Anarchist Group. We held business meetings in the hall in Wilson Street, ironically adjacent to the pub called 'The Hangman's Rest'. It was here, each week, the propaganda meetings were arranged, all on a voluntary basis. Some would elect to travel to Edinburgh or Paisley or Hamilton. Edinburgh meetings were held in the Mound. In Paisley the meetings were held in the Square at Gilmour Street railway station. Occasionally meetings were held on weekdays in Paisley, and also in Glasgow in Drury Street and Rose Street. Every week meetings were held outside work gates: outside Yarrow's and Elderslie Dry Dock; outside John Brown's shipyard; Blythswood shipyard; Dalmuir Ordinance Factory; Fairfield's shipyard. Dennis McGlynn, a Clydebank comrade, was well accepted at John Brown's, he being a local lad. Eddie Shaw was always well received at Yarrow's.

Eddie resided in Bridgeton and there were many of Yarrow's workers who came from Bridgeton, Calton, Partick and Govan: they could understand and always delighted in Eddie's brand of humour put over in the real speech of the Glasgow streets. This was Anarchism in the language they were best acquainted with and they loved it.

Eddie was one of the 'old School' who never went to jail for opposing the war.

Jimmy Dick speaking at Anarchist meeting, Brunswick Street, 1945.

He was apprehended for failing to attend for medical examination (medical assassination, Eddie called it) and when he was out on bail he consulted Guy Aldred who advised him that there was a difference between being ordered to report on a specified day and being ordered to report on a specified day at a specified time. No specified time had been stated. On the day Eddie had been ordered to report, the authorities, knowing their man, had jumped the gun. They had apprehended him whilst in theory he still had time to report. Eddie appealed at the High Court and incredibly his appeal was upheld. He was acquitted and awarded £10 expenses. In a matter of months the upper age-limit for consciption was lowered, so Eddie escaped his 'medical assassination'. Jimmy Raeside, Charlie Baird, Roger Carr, Dennis McGlynn, Jimmy Dick and others had all been forced to accept the hospitality of the Crown in Barlinnie. It was no deterrent to them. And on their release their zeal for the cause was undiminished.

The Anarchist hall in Wilson Street was a refuge for conscientious objectors and soldiers absent without leave who claimed to be Anarchist sympathisers. We didn't care whether they were genuine sympathisers or not. They were working-class and trying to escape the war. That was enough. A key hung on a string from inside the letter box and anybody could get access any time by just inserting a hand and raising the key.

Four of us linked ourselves to the Glasgow Anarchist Group after the Apprentices' Strike. A while later I joined a ship at Rothesay Dock in Yoker as an engineer.

When I got back home after that first voyage two of my old friends had drifted away but one was still with the group. That was Bill Johnson. After a year or so began to dabble more in trade union activities. He was becoming ambitious for a place in the trade union hierarchy. He is now and has been for some years Lord Provost of Clydebank. This is not any condemnation of Anarchism. It is a condemnation of Bill Johnson. Even people calling themselves Anarchists can be opportunists. You have to look at the man as well as the 'ism'.

In a certain sense the Glasgow Anarchists of that period made a unique contribution to the broad Anarchist movement in Britain. Most of the comrades could accept the philosophy of Egoism and dovetail it into the Syndicalist tendency within the movement. For my part I was quite strong about this fusion. In fact I think I was a firmer adherent of this school than was Eddie Shaw although, as I say, initially Eddie was the teacher and I was the pupil. Many were admirers of Kropotkin as I was. Kropotkin did of course criticise the philosophy of Egoism. In spite of this, I do not think Kropotkin's 'Mutual Aid' really contradicts Stirner's argument. It is at least obvious to me that those who practice mutual aid are in fact the best egoists. This view is not a reconciliation; it is a fusion. Kropotkin is not I, and I am not Kropotkin. Stirner is not I nor am I

:irner. Both are dead: I subdue their arguments if they want to argue. I
ominate my thought: I am not its slave. I am neither a Kropotkinite nor a
:irnerite nor any other 'ite' or 'ist'. This, in the main, was the healthy attitude of
ost of the Glasgow Anarchists of the period.

Guy Aldred was not exactly endeared to the Syndicalists, although many of
e Wilson Street Anarchists, such as Rab Lyle from Burnbank, were frequent
sitors to the Strickland Press and had a lot of time for Guy. Nevertheless the
dustrial expression of Anarchism was conspicuous by its absence in Guy's
aper 'The Word'. Most of the content of 'The Word' was anti-parliamentarian,
ati-militarist and pacifist. Guy was an intellectual. His background was clerical
ad he had no real contact with, or profound knowledge of, the industrial
orkplace. He failed to recognise that those Syndicalists who worked during the
ar in industries producing war potential did not live in a social vacuum. What
out farmers and land workers in general? They were also sucked into the war
fort. Even Napoleon knew an army only marches on a full belly.

A strong Syndicalist movement could have taken over the fields, factories and
orkshops and all the means of communication, for the benefit of the mass of
e people. That's what we were about. The only place it was ever likely to
appen was at the point of production. We were certain of that much. Then the
orizontal war and the vertical war could have been ended. What do I mean? The
orizontal war is war between different so-called nations. When this war ends,
e vertical war continues: the war between the haves and the have-nots.
orizontal wars are only State-promoted diversions from the real war which is
ways vertical.

Guy had had long-standing problems, probably more to do with clashes of
ersonality than anything else, with the Freedom Press group in London.
uring the war the Anarchist paper 'Freedom' changed its name to 'War
ommentary'. In 1945 four comrades from the editorial board were charged
th sedition: attempting to cause disaffection within the armed services. It
emmed from an article in 'War Commentary' in which it was urged that the
med forces should retain their weapons after the war to assist in the
volutionary struggle – the vertical war. The Glasgow Anarchists organised
otest meetings in defence of the four. We rented the Cosmo cinema and
other – I think it was called the Grand – which was next door to the Locarno
allroom. Both cinemas were packed to capacity.

Speakers came along from other organisations to lend their support. Oliver
own from the Scottish Nationalists was there. Jimmy Raeside, representing
e Glasgow Anarchists spoke in the Grand. Eddie Shaw was on the platform, or
age if you like, in the Cosmo. I remember Eddie making a joke about this. "The
ommical Party" (the Communist Party), he quipped, "always said I should be
comedian on the stage: now they at least should be happy to see me up here."

The CP, needless to say, hated Eddie's guts, he having humiliated them in debate too many times.

Sadly, Guy Aldred gave no support whatsoever. He was still unable to put aside his deep-rooted personal conflict with some members of the Freedom Press group. Well, everybody has shortcomings in the eyes of someone. Guy was no exception, great fighter for social justice though he was.

Three of the accused were found guilty and sentenced to twelve months imprisonment. The fourth, Italian-born Marie Louise Berneri, was discharged. She and one of her co-accused, Vernon Richards, had entered into a marriage of convenience to save her being interned as an alien. In the eyes of the law this made Vernon responsible for his wife's conduct, and she was discharged on these grounds.

I would like to apologise to all comrades still living who were involved with the group at that period. I am conscious that I haven't given the group its just reward either individually or collectively. I earnestly hope some truly honest working-class historian will one day render to posterity a greater insight into the important contribution made by the Glasgow Anarchists. There is no greater wealth than knowing the story of how some people sincerely endeavoured to demolish the insane asylum the State has penned us in. I leave this as a signpost only, indicating the road we took and some of the thoughts we had on the way.

R. D. LAING

from 'Wisdom, Madness and Folly'

CAN A PSYCHIATRIC institution exist for 'really' psychotic people where there is communication within *solidarity,* community and communion, instead of the It-district, the no-man's-land between staff and patients?

This rift or rent in solidarity may be healed *in* a professional therapeutic relationship. A 'relationship', professional or otherwise, which does not heal this rent can hardly be called therapeutic since it seems to me that what is professionally called a 'therapeutic relationship' cannot exist without a primary human camaraderie being present and manifest. If it is not there to start with, therapy will have been successful if it is there before it ends.

There can be no solidarity if a basic, primary, fellow human feeling of being together has been lost or is absent. It is not easy to retain this feeling when you press the button. Very seldom, when I pressed the button, could I feel I was doing for this chap in terrible mental agony what I hoped he would do for me if I had his mind and brains and he had mine.

This issue of solidarity and camaraderie between me as a doctor and those patients did not arise for me, it did not occur to me until I was in the British Army, a psychiatrist and a lieutenant, sitting in padded cells in my own ward with completely psychotic patients, doomed to deep insulin and electric shocks in the middle of the night. For the first time it dawned on me that it was almost impossible for a patient to be a pal or for a patient to have a snowball's chance in hell of finding a comrade in me.

It would be a mistake to suppose that 'mental' institutions are It-districts. There may be a lot of camaraderie between staff and staff, and patients and patients. But there tends to be an It-district between staff and patients. Why this should be so may not be immediately apparent. But when one looks into it one sees that it can hardly be otherwise, under the circumstances.

All communication occurs on the basis either of strife, camaraderie or confusion. There can be communication without communion. This is the norm. There is very little communion in many human transactions. The greatest danger facing us, the human species, is ourselves. We are not at peace with one another.

We are at strife, not in communion.

The New Year is the biggest celebration in Scotland. It is marked by prolonged carousing on the part of the alcoholic fraternity, but many teetotallers celebrate the spirit of the New Year contentedly sober. There is no 'religion' about it. There is a special spirit abroad – 'Auld Lang Syne', 'A man's a man for a' that.' In Gartnavel, in the so-called 'back wards', I have seen catatonic patients who hardly make a move, or utter a word, or seem to notice or care about anyone or anything around them year in and year out, smile, laugh, shake hands, wish someone 'A guid New Year' and even dance...and then by the afternoon or evening or next morning revert to their listless apathy. The change, however fleeting, in some of the most chronically withdrawn, 'backward' patients is amazing. If any drug had this effect, for a few hours, even minutes, it would be world famous, and would deserve to be celebrated as much as the Scottish New Year. The intoxicant here however is not a drug, not even alcoholic spirits, but the celebration of a spirit of fellowship.

There are interfaces in the socio-economic-political structure of our society where communion is impossible or almost impossible. We are ranged on opposite sides. We are enemies, we are against each other before we meet. We are so far apart as not to recognise the other even as a human being or, if we do, only as one to be abolished immediately.

This rift or rent occurs between master and slave, the wealthy and the poor, on the basis of such differences as class, race, sex, age.

It crops up also across the sane-mad line. It occurred to me that it might be a relevant factor in some of the misery and disorder of certain psychotic processes; even sometimes, possibly, a salient factor in aetiology, care, treatment, recovery or deterioration.

This rift or rent is healed through a relationship with anybody, but it has to be somebody. Any 'relationship' through which this fracture heals is 'therapeutic', whether it is what is called, professionally, a 'therapeutic relationship' or not. The loss of a sense of human solidarity and camaraderie and communion affects people in different ways. Some people never seem to miss it. Others can't get on without it. It was not easy to retain this feeling when I pressed the button to give someone an electric shock if I could not feel I was doing to him what I hoped he would do for me if I had his brains and he mine. I gave up 'pressing the button'.

ALEX CATHCART

Nostalgically Speaking, Imagination is Money

AT HER WINDOW, high above the Merchant City of Glasgow, Charlotte looked out. She saw a silver moon set in a dark blue sky with twinkling stars. She could hear the steps of the tobacco barons in their buckled shoes, hear them as they talked of their ships due in from the colonies, and without listening too hard she could almost hear them sneeze as they sniffed up their snuff and clacked shut their little silver snuff boxes. Dark sky, silver moon, twinkling stars, and the old Glasgow and its people she could see in her mind's eye – how she longed to write about that. There was a time it would have been possible. But Charlotte had traded her gift for the salary and the car and the prestige of being a Public Relations Officer with British Telecom. If there was guilt in her feelings on an evening like this, there was also a terrible sense of loss. And there was also anger.

Charlotte turned a little and looked back into the room. David still sat in his boucled leather armchair, the one he loved, the one he had rescued when his boss threatened to throw it out. He was poring over some client's papers. How strange, thought Charlotte, that a person in such a dry-as-dust job as Investments Analyst could live with such a latent romantic as herself. Perhaps it was because they were opposite they co-habited so well. Charlotte had wanted to get married – David pointed out the tax advantages, Charlotte had wanted a cottage in the country – David had pointed to the desirability of future profit-taking based upon the rising house price potential in the Merchant City. Yet underneath it all, Charlotte was sure David was a romantic, somewhere.

In the full moon and the clear night, and far over, Charlotte could just make out the silhouette of the statue of John Knox set high on his plinth, overlooking the Merchants Graveyard. She had been in that graveyard once, years ago. One fine summer's day she had climbed its hill, stood at John Knox's monument, and looked over the whole of the City, but the view had been spoiled then by the smoke from the factories and the shipyards and the graveyard peace had been disturbed by men in brown overalls as they worked in the brewery below. The factories were away now, maybe another walk up might be worth a look. Might be able to see the Garden Festival from up there. Should be able to see the big Loop-the-Loop at least. Fantastic how they put whole train loads of people through these loops and hoops, so fast. So fast they could only yell and giggle as it happened to them.

Charlotte felt the moon and the stars work their wonders, drawing her up, until she was wrapped around by the blue blanket sky, suspended, as Lois Lane was suspended in the first Superman film. From up, amongst the sky, she could look down and see it all, see it all laid out in the model in the Real Estate Agent's office, only more real, more alive. There, over there, there was the bridge where William Wallace had led his men into Glasgow; and there, there was where Bonnie Prince Charlie had stayed as he waited for his tribute. There was the Green where the weavers had rioted, and where Glasgow's first Trade Union people had met. And there was the court-house the rent-strikers had put under siege in 1914. That siege which had threatened to overthrow a government, and had won a Bill to provide council housing for the people. Looking, it was easy to see the crowds surrounding the court-house, cheer the women who led while their men were at war, and cry as their leaders were set free by order of the English Parliament. Charlotte felt excited and knew she could write this into a good book about a man fighting at the front while his wife fought at home and he would be brave and she would be brave and he would win a medal and arrive home after being posted missing just in time to see her freed and they would kiss and all the people would get nice new homes in the country.

Further over she could see George Square where her father had told her there had once been machine-guns aimed against the people.

Charlotte stepped away from the window.

"David. David. Are you finished?"

David clicked his pen. "Almost darling. I'm just entering a free competition. I'm increasing my Banker's Order to the Labour Party. Goes into a free draw, gives me the chance to win a free, signed photograph of Neil."

Charlotte smiled. This was another reason why she had fallen for David – his quiet radicalism. David never spoke much about his membership of the Labour Party, or his politics at all, really. Only now and again, when he'd been mixing gin with his pints of lager, would she hear him mumble and mutter to some old University crony words like, 'Gramsci', or, 'bloody London boroughs'. But he only teased her and laughed a little when she spoke up for David Owen. He was liberal enough in that way. Charlotte crossed over and kneeled beside the chair, touching his thigh. The pile of paper looked impressive. Charlotte thumbed through the corners of the pile. "That was a lot of work to bring home."

"Yes. It was. No alternative, really. Black Monday. Given us all a few headaches, Charlotte."

"Mmm."

"Oh. Reminds me. Might not be any bonus this year, so we may just have to look at our projections for next year all over again."

"No bonus? And you're still bringing work home? David, you're too, too..." The *mot juste* was escaping. "...too loyal."

David kissed her on the forehead. "It's not for the Company, darling. Not really. It's for all those little people out there that invested in equities instead of trusts. They're only ordinary folk like you and me. That's what I bring work home for. I'm afraid they jumped in on a Bull market, and were a teensy bit over-exposed when it turned to the big bad Bear. But if I can help them, I will."

"David. And here I am nagging you too. Tell you what, let's go out tonight. Oh, come on. We'll go downstairs to 'The Wee Peever Bed'."

David gave her another of those nice kisses on the forehead. "Now there's an idea."

Charlotte and David simply slung on their plain blousons, Charlotte tying a silk scarf around her neck, before casually shoving it up onto her right shoulder.

As Charlotte waited for David to lock the locks and put on the infra-red, she looked along the narrow corridor. Someone at the far end had put out a small table with a potted plant on top. "Oh, David, look at that. Maybe we could do that. Takes the bare look off the concrete."

"Mmm. Suppose so."

They went downstairs, out through the security door, and crossed the narrow, newly cobbled street, and went into The Wee Peever Bed pub.

The customers at the bar were tightly bunched in groups at either end. No-one leaned on the centre portion of the brass rail that ran the length of the dark wooden counter. The rail gleamed like a tube of pure gold. David and Charlotte looked at each other and laughed. Tonight was Peever Night.

They took the only table available, set in the corner of the raised section. A waiter came to them. Across his arm hung a white towel with two red stripes down its middle between which were the words: Glasgow Corporation Baths. He handed over the menu-card. This week it was the one that looked like the lid of an old shoe-polish tin. The waiter was a new chap. He waited. The man was a bit on the small side. This made his grey flannel short trousers come a little lower than the usual mid-leg. His grey, tattered woollen jersey had its two buttons open at the top, and two long hairs peeked out from his throat. The black socks with the white rings were pulled down over his clumpy boots. One of the boots had its toecap torn free and it pointed upward. "Anything to drink?" the man asked. "Two Perrier water, please" answered David. Charlotte nodded as the man looked at her. The worn-out toecap flapped as the man walked away, brushing a hand through his hair, which was cut short as though with a bowl to guide the shearer.

David held up his menu-card and spoke to Charlotte without looking at her. "I know that lad."

"Who? Him? The waiter?"

"Yeh. Worked in Scott Lithgow's shipyard with my older brother. Welder I think he was."

"Was he? Really? Must say he's waiting as though he's done it all his life."

"Adaptability, Charlotte. Key to success nowadays. Got to invest your money and talents in the coming things. Like this," he waved a hand around, "Nostalgia. Money in this game today, you know. Must agree though. The man looks the part. What you having?"

"Oh, I don't know, Chucky Stane soup looks attractice."

"That's just kidney beans."

"Oh know-all. As if I didn't know. I'll just have a main course: Lits de Peever a Maitre."

"Yeh. I've had that before, It's good actually. O.K., well I'll try the Hopscotch Pie, and follow with some, eh, Caramel d'Un Franc."

The waiter returned with their drinks and took the order. As the man wrote, David tried to converse. "You're new aren't you?"

The man nodded, but did not look up from his writing.

"What do they call you then?"

"Jimmy"

"Oh."

"That's it?"

"That'll do for now thanks."

Charlotte leaned over. "Talkative, wasn't he?" David shrugged.

The cutlery was set out by a girl dressed in a pink dress made in some kind of satin material. Charlotte thought that the mud-stains on the front were quite tastefully arranged. In the girl's hair was loosely tied white ribbon, which had a longer trailing end which dangled over her forehead. David ordered Beaujolais.

The male waiter brought the meals, and from somewhere Glenn Miller music began. The place was pretty full for a week-night. Some couples came in, stood just inside the door, looked, and went out again.

As Dave and Charlotte finished their meal, the lights round the edge of the bar and restaurant areas dimmed, leaving only a rectangle of bright light shining down in front of the bar counter. People at the front of the bar lifted their drinks and moved. Some were asked to move by Jimmy. These tables and chairs were pulled back. On the floor, in the space under the light, was the Peever Bed, set out on the tiles. Three lines of three square boxes, white-edged, as if done by the traditional pipe clay, while the semi-circular boundary around the number 10 at the top was done in great whorls of pink. The waitress in the pink dress came forward, knelt in front of the centre-row of boxes. The numbers were painted yellow, 1, 2, 3. To claps and shouts the girl rubbed her peeverstane on the floor, backwards and forwards, then let it go. It slid easily into box 1. The girl hopped in after it and began hitting the stane into all the boxes, and hopping after it. In box 10 she leaned over from her hopping position, lifting her free leg up high behind her. The young bucks cheered. One or two or three knelt down behind her, shouting. The girl carried on. She reached fivesie. Each time she lifted her leg up, more cheers came. When she reached sixie, the man called Jimmy slid his

ever into box 1, and began hopping around, taking care not to interfere with
e girl, who carried on, timing her hops to miss his. But Jimmy fell. The
ustomers cheered.

After fifteen minutes the employees stopped playing, and the customers took
ver, hopping and falling, and laughing as they lay. Some kicked their legs in the
r as they lay.

Why don't you have a go, David?"

Who me? Oh no. Not me. Anyway from what I can see the fun is to do it when
ou're drunk."

One man captured the attention of the crowd. Dressed in a white jacket and
ack tight trousers, he was hopping with style, standing erect on one leg,
olding his arms up straight, high, while scowling at the peever bed.

Looks like a cross between John Travolta and a matador, don't you think?"
id Charlotte.

Maybe. I think it's the jacket though."

The wine was finished. David inclined his head. Charlotte nodded. He
gnalled the waitress with some difficulty. Her attention was on John Jose
ravolta. But at last she came over. David paid by Visa. He did not tip. Often he
ad stopped Charlotte from tipping, telling her that the only way to get Glasgow
ourism going was to drag it away from the attitudes of servility rampant in the
rvice sector, and epitomised by the eager acceptance of tips. Charlotte knew it
as really just him and his politics again. She knew Socialists did not give tips.
avid was looking at his watch. "I think we should go, Charlotte. We've got
ork in the morning, remember."

O.K., but I know you're just after my body."

Oh not tonight, darling. I'm pretty tired."

Oh we'll see."

No seeing about it. I'm really tired."

They left just as another customer fell flat on his back and guffawed, while the
owd cheered. The man called Jimmy did not return David's nod. Outside, a
etness had settled over the tops of the cobbles. David fell. Charlotte laughed
nd hauled him up. "Maybe you should have tried the peever after all." she said.
avid said nothing. At the security door Charlotte drew David's attention to the
ames behind the little slits of light. "Did you see that one, David? That's a new
ne."

Sorry to disappoint you, Charlotte. That name's been there well over a month
ow."

Oh."

Once upstairs and finally in, Charlotte made them both hot chocolate. When
was ready she found that David was already in bed, his bedside reading lamp
ulled over to shine on the book he was balancing on his knees. Charlotte
orried about the duvet cover as he took the chocolate clumsily. The design was

taken from a nineteenth century document. A stain would really spoil it.

"Thanks" said David. He jabbed a finger on the book. "This De Lorean was some man, you know. I mean even allowing everything. Quite a deicision-maker."

"Was he?" The tone made David look, but he did not pursue anything.

Charlotte undressed, putting her clothes neatly into their little shelf-boxes in the old plain wardrobe they had bought at an auction and had painted white. The long strips of tape had been David's idea, and although one or two strips were turning up at the ends they did make it kind of Mackintoshy. Settling herself into bed, Charlotte leaned over, picking up her mug of chocolate, and cupped it in both hands. She sipped and stared in the far-off kind of way.

"David?"

"Mmm?"

"Do you think I could write a book about a Glasgow pirate captain that comes back to his home in the old quarter and finds his wife playing peever like that girl – only in a really rough tavern with lots of bad types about – and discovers she's under the influence of the local gambler, or something?"

David pushed his lamp away, lay down, stretched out, turned it off, leaving Charlotte in her own light. "Charlotte, there is no doubt about it. You're living in the best part of Glasgow for atmosphere. I must say it certainly seems to be stimulating your imagination. A story like that should make a bomb. Goodnight, Charlotte."

Charlotte placed her chocolate on the bedside table, and turned her light off. Outside, through the bedroom window, she could see the silver moon, and the dark blue sky, and a few twinkling stars.

DOMINIC BEHAN

Call Me Comrade

ABOUT FORTY YEARS ago in Ruchill, me and Freddie Anderson and Matt McGinn were waiting for the revolution. It was a favourite pastime of the 'dissident' mind. We were young and sincere and we knew the importance of being earnest. Oh God, we knew that alright. Worse than which we wrote it all down. Lenin had called for all youth to sing its way to freedom, so we sang our songs, and brought to the masses our prophecy of the new world to come. Within the tenement closes, most decent working men, weighed down, one could perceive, with the dignity of Labour, came to their doors, eyed us and our fraternal message, and promptly told us to 'Fuck off'.

This was called 'serving our time to the revolution' and it was quite unlikely to do anybody any harm, unless we caught pneumonia. It hadn't if the truth be known, been doing anybody any harm for years. Well, give or take a few people hanged here or there, who would have been treated so had they never protested.

You don't believe me? What about the Lad frae Ayr, who instead of wearing the knees out of his breeks, suffered from shabby flies? There was Keir Hardie who took his politics from Scotia to London, and, when he tried to take them back to Scotland, the folk from Cumnock cried, 'Oh for fuck sake!', or words to that effect.

And yet London seemed to be the place. Ever since Ramsay MacDonald, the folk in the Labour Party had come to believe that the only socialism for Scotland was the colonial variety. And what with Manny Shinwell and Davey Kirkwood, could you blame them for their views? Well was it said by John Maclean about those two worthies, that they'd be addressed as 'Sir' long before they'd be called Saint.

The trouble with me and Freddy and Matt was that we were curious about what went on inside the covers of books. There was Charlie Marx on this and Freddie Engels on that and an Indian gentleman from London called R. Palm Dutt was supposed to interpret them for us. Well, I needn't tell you that we were able to read as well as any other colonial.

That's what started all the trouble, I think. Me and Freddie and Matt, noticing that the comrades in London had made a mistake in their all embracing philosophies, went to London to put the matter to rights. At King Street we asked to see the leader to point out that the 'British Road to Socialism' said nothing about Maclean or self determination. And that grand old Scottish rebel, Peter Kerrigan, who had fought for the Spanish Republic, met us at the door and said 'Fuck off you chauvinist anti-British bastards!'.

But we were not the first to be treated with such Anglo-Saxon incivilities and chance was that we wouldn't be the last. The Skirving shoemaker, Thomas Hardy, founded the London Correspondence Society and brought Scottish republicanism to England. Alexander Skirving founded the United Scotsmen and, when arrested with other clergymen, friends, took Scottish republicanism to Australia. Arrested at the same time was the young Scottish barrister, Thomas Muir. When freed from assisted passage to Botany Bay by George Washington and Tom Paine, Muir introduced Scottish republicanism to France.

The only ones, apparently, who didn't want to know about Scottish republicanism, were the Scots. And the situation hadn't changed a great deal when, two hundred years later, me and Matt and Freddie, regardless of the danger to our sanity, went on the knocker, preached our message, and enjoyed the fairly unanimous hostility of the masses. And still the revolution never came.

But how the hell could it? Had we not been told by Willie Gallagher that the cause was only for men born sober and stiff? Had Harry McShane not insisted that the only way to unity was through dissent? And did our old friend Norrie Buchan not swear that nationalism was next to nihilism in the eyes of the Third Red International? So meself and Matt and Freddie, realising that since it was the voice of the Holy Trinity in King Street in Triplicate, listened.

I blame all the confusion on misleading metaphors. People had been talking about what they called the 'broad church politic'. And so we had been reared, you see, not to question the sacred mysteries. Therefore, when somebody like Johnny Gollan told us that the real leader of the Scottish revolutionaries was a Yorkshireman called Harry Pollit who thought that Alba was the north of England, we didn't, for the sake of unity, question that. The same sacrifice for unity, comrades, has given me a severe pain in the Erse for years. And we only knew one answer. Me and Matt and Freddie went back and knocked a little harder.

Scotland itself was not very encouraging of our efforts. We wanted, like Mayakovsky, to favour the poets, but the poets made it damned difficult. That decent man, Hamish Henderson, was a paid up member of the Italian

Communist Party. Dear Morris Blythsman confused the slogan 'On to the Republic' with the cry, 'No Surrender!'. Our great Sidney Goodsir Smith seemed to owe allegiance to William Wallace, which, though highly commendable from an historical point of view, wasn't very practical when every comrade was needed on the knocker.

Nor should it be thought that sitting around waiting for the revolution was an easy billet in the class war. In those days everything was more expectation and desire than hope. After all, the whole of Alba was the bastion of the Tory Party, and the Scottish Labour M.P.s were as scarce in Westminster as trades unionists in the U.D.M. But, if we did not as yet possess the key, we at least had the knocker – Freddie, and me, and Matt McGinn.

And then it happened. Almost as MacDiarmid said it would, 'by stealth'. Nothing had been changed quite utterly. No terrible beauty yet. But, as soon as we could find enough elected socialists to get out from under the remains of the empire. Overnight, almost, there weren't enough parliamentary Tories to fill a decent sized polling booth. Tartania was suddenly the tip of an isthmus, and the gang of four had become the 'Sloane Ranger'. Although I never noticed it until quite recently, a revolution has taken place, comrades. It must have been while me and Freddie and Matt were on the knocker.

*   *   *

As to poetry. I have earned my living as a professional and full-time writer for close on forty years. My influences are from the dialectical poets of Ireland and Scotland, mainly MacNeice, MacDiarmid, Hamish Henderson and Sydney Goodsir Smith. But I do not stem, as it were, from that tradition. One look at my work will show you that, like an anarchist with rules, I accept what suits me from conventionality and reject the rest.

I am not particularly interested in the length of a poem. Be it as short or as long as it will; I accept Ben Johnson's criterion:

> Even one alone verse sometimes makes a perfect poem.

I am from the working class, but I am not a 'working-class' writer. I have never met one, no more than I have met a 'middle-class' writer or an 'upper-class' writer. Naturally enough I understand the condition of the working class, and if I didn't want to do something about changing it there would be something greatly lacking in me.

I like certain poets and dislike others. Mostly I dislike those who exhibit a preference for establishment values and betray an ignorance of society as it is constituted. I have a particular dislike for the so-called poets of the obscure since I fail to see why, if the first job of the writer is to communicate, anybody should ever indulge in symbols other than the characters of words – letters.

'Babylon' just illustrates the luxurious childhood I enjoyed amidst the tenements.

Babylon

Kitty Collins lost her drawers,
Won't you kindly lend her yours.
Two long men, four long feet
Walking down Cathedral Street.

Swiftly, on a young man's song
Came the road to Babylon,
Finding fairy fields more wide
Than those in which old minds abide.

Richer far in memory
Than youth ever seemed to be.
So the song that nature meant
By laughing long in tenements.

Would you like to follow me
Through a slum's eternity,
Stair by stair and floor by floor,
Swiftly by each hungry door?

The smell is what one must expect
When humankind is tightly packed
Into such beleagured truth
That passes for my erstwhile youth.

Was it here my childish sobs
When Little Neil was snatched by God?
While hating Scrooge for Tiny Tim,
I should have prayed to be like him.

Prayers were few and seldom told,
'Sweet God, it's warm', or 'Christ it's cold!'
Relentlessly the Rosary
Reminder that mortality
Though kept at bay by talk of Lourdes,
Was most unlikely to be cured.

No bread from fishes here, you'll find.
The blind that are around stay blind.
And even mangy Lazarus
Would be the man of most of us
Poverty is not at all
The stuff of which a miracle.

'Suffer them to come to me'
Was but for death in infancy.
A mournful crime when children die
A druids stand to sanctify.

But what festive turn it takes
At yours, or someone else's wake?
Like Maggie Carr when she lay dead
And Mary Reilly's maidenhead
Was taken in this very house
By Mrs Carr's lamenting spouse.
They held poor Mary all to blame
And wept for he whose kingdom came.

From that sad landing window wide
Leapt Mrs Duffy's suicide.
She flew a moment e'er she fell
To where the priest decided, 'hell'.
I watched and wept, quite openly,
The neighbours sought to comfort me,
And swore I was the nicest boy
Who could for Mrs Duffy cry.
But grown-ups never know what fears
Give rise to childhood's bitter tears,
When that old Biddy failed to float,
She landed on my paper boat.

'Oh gentle Jesus, meek and mild

WORKERS CITY

Come to me a little child',
Was but one prayer we children said
When kneel' ng by untidy beds.

In that room there, that two-per   nt,
Through fingered eyes the stars I'd c unt.
Then shameful of such reverie
I'd beg Our Lord to come to me.
And, more in horror than in prayer,
I'd peek to see if He was there!
Oh frightening Jesus, in the dark,
And in your hand that bleeding heart!

On that top lobby, by that door,
I lay quite naked on the floor
With Rita Reilly in her skin.
The two of us did dirty things
I mind that assignation fine
For she was eight and I was nine.

From down below a latin chant
Sweet inungere sacrament
Went out to God to spare a boy
Who might from meningitis die.
The praying must have done the trick,
He lived, a raving lunatic.

Did I say prayers were seldom said?
Just shows what stays within the head.
O Salutaris Hostia, the word of God. Apocrypha
That passes for philosophy
In men of simple piety.
But, how could we endure the slum
Without the tender opium?

Ubi bene, Gloria,
Uni tres nos qui Domino!
And, armed with phrases such as these
We rose, triumphant, to our knees.

This house has mansions by the score,
In each one bides the noble poor

Who hide in hollow ornaments
The signs of paupered violence,
Provvy checks and pawnshop chits,
Marriage lines and bailiff's writs!

And brave they lie for clergy lied
That poverty's a badge of pride!
Do they allow such 'dignity'
To bide within the presbytery?

Was this your meaning when you slung
The bankers all to Kingdom Come?
Do poor men in your House belong
Or is it all a holy con?

How many ways to liberty?
Christ, when will end eternity?
Sweet simple Jesus, hear my song.
How many miles to Babylon?

THURSO BERWICK
(1919-1981)

IN THE ANTI-POLARIS campaign of the early sixties, Thurso Berwick (Morris Blythman) wrote many memorable and hard-hitting songs against the American nuclear presence in Scotland. His best known song is perhaps 'The Glesca Eskimoes', written in collaboration with T. S. Law, in tumultuous mockery of hapless Captain Laning, of U.S. submarine Proteus, who described the demonstrators paddling their little canoes round his all-powerful nuclear bombs as 'a bunch of eskimoes'. To the tune of the Glasgow Orange song, 'The Billy Boys', the chorus sherrecks:

> Hullo! Hullo! We are the Eskimoes.
> Hullo! Hullo! The Glesca Eskimoes.
> We'll gaff that nyaff ca'd Lanin,
> We'll spear him where he blows,
> We are the Glesca Eskimoes.

In a later song, 'The Eskimo Republic', again to an Orange tune, The Boys of Garvagh, we can share Morris's utopian vision of a free Scotland: and through his famous 'contrived banality', the comical and the bizarre, with pure Glasgow-style humour, he says it all.

The Eskimo Republic

Now fortune's wheel it is birlan roon
An nation's rise that yince were doon,
So it's time tae sing a rebel tune
For the Eskimo Republic.

Chorus:
Whaur there is nae class, there is nae boss,
Nae kings nir queens, an damn the loss,
An ye get boozed up for a six months doss
In the Eskimo Republic.

When they mak a law, sure they aa agree,
For they aa sit on the com-mit-tee,
An they've got nae Lords an nae M.P.s
In the Eskimo Republic.

Now the Eskimo's no like me and you.
Every Eskimo has his ain i-ga-loo
An his mither-in-law has an i-ga-loo too
In the Eskimo Republic.

O, they flee aboot in thir wee kayaks
An they stick harpoons intae whales' backs.
Then they cut them up intae tasty wee snacks
For the Eskimo Republic.

When an Eski wean goes tae Eski school,
He sits up nice on an Eski stool
An he sings an he laughs an he learns the rules
O the Eskimo Republic.

Now thir fitbaa gemmes are aa clean an fair
An the crowd's aa pals wi the fitbaa players
Cos the park is patrolled by -- polar bears
In the Eskimo Republic.

When an Eskimo sings an Eski sang,
He gies it the real auld Eski twang
An his favourite wan is 'I belang
Tae the Eskimo Republic'.

Now the Eskimo is geyan gallus
An his i-ga-loo is his ain wee palace
An it's aa lit up by the Aurora Borealis
In the Eskimo Republic.

IAN McKECHNIE

The Balloon Goes Up

He brushed his teeth again and he could still taste it, at least he thought he could. Toothpaste snaked over the wash-basin and on the floor, and his hands were still shaking.

"The Prime Minister on the phone, Sir."

"Christ," he thought, looking in the mirror, "this looks fucking comical."

His mouth was wreathed in toothpaste foam. The aide's face, reflected a look of amused puzzlement.

"What's so fucking funny?" he screamed.

Suds spluttered from his mouth over the mirror and wash-basin. The aide jumped from sight. It was obvious what was funny. He was hysterical and he knew it. Objectivity was part of his hysteria.

He rinsed out his mouth and dried his face. Toothpaste was smeared in his moustache.

"This," he thought, "is a Keystone Comedy."

He walked out of the bathroom still towelling his face and picked up the telephone.

"Yes Ma'am."

It was the school matron voice. Soothing and clinical. The one matron used as you winced when she dressed your cuts and grazes.

On the T.V. the day's events were being replayed.

"Yes Ma'am," he had cancelled tomorrow's engagements.

"No Ma'am," he hadn't yet seen a doctor.

"Yes Ma'am," he would let the doctor look at him.

The voice kept on. Ten years now. Does the bitch ever stop?

On the T.V. he was going through the motions again.

Cutting the ribbon, declaring another Yuppieville well and truly open, the balloons going up to orchestrated applause and then he stoppped speaking, the T.V. fixing his attention.

The balloons went up.

One of the balloons, a red one, detached itself from the main flight, described an arc and burst on his head.

He was in and out of the memory, the taste of petrol in his mouth and the shivering terror.

He saw and remembered himself being rushed, blinded, into the flats, the bodyguards shouting, shoving him, holding him at arms length, taking no chances.

There was the possibility of fire.

A white-faced citizen was being hauled from the crowd, a man in his fifties, dressed in a shabby blue anorak, grimacing or grinning? as his arms were twisted behind him.

"The bastard!" he said, dropping the phone.

He turned and made for the bathroom, fear bringing up the taste.

The aide retrieved the phone and made stammering apologies to a shrill small voice.

He entered the bathroom and closed the door, then wearily, he sat down on the toilet and covered his face with his fists.

"The bastard!", he repeated, knowing now with certainty the attack was merely to frighten.

He began to weep, feeling sorry for himself. He was very tired and he had been badly frightened and the world had seen his terror and embarrassment.

"The bastards! The fucking bastards!"

He began to shiver.

Petrol.

The taste was back.

He would have to wash his mouth out again.

JEFF TORRINGTON

Singing: No, No, Yuppie, Yuppie – NO!

IN EARLY JANUARY, 1968, when the country was being run by a Gannex raincoat which any political pawnbroker would have rejected as being urgently in need of Socialist re-proofing, a hurricane, code-named 'Low Q', struck Central Scotland, causing a score of deaths, rendering hundreds homeless, and inflicting severe structural damage. How many trees were lost on that wild night was at the time of small public interest. But, such was not the case last October when a similar hurricane blasted some blue chip counties in Southern England. On that occasion arboreal destruction was of prime concern. The Observer magazine, for example, in a review of 1987 reported that the English storm "Felled 15 million tress and killed 19 people..."

That the focus of contemporary concern should be on material rather than on human loss is in keeping with the pernicious yahoo values that pollute these Ethicless Eighties. In the Filofaxical world of the City, trees represent long-term investment, whereas ordinary humans (at present being reprogrammed for drudgery in the Service Sector) belong, financially speaking, to quick put-through expedience-capitalism.

This was not yet the case back in the Glasgow of the Sixties. On that bleak January dawn which followed 'the night of the flying lums' Glasgow's Lord Provost boldly declared that not a single workman would pass through his own gates to tend to his storm damage until every household in the city had been made watertight. This went down well with his wind-blitzed citizens, although a malicious rumour circulated that the City Father's property had been repaired that same night when a squad of Corporation tradesmen was lowered onto his roof by helicopter.

During those debris-strewn days, Ross 'n' Mabon (not the comedy team once so popular in the Old Queens, but the Scottish Secretary and Under Sec. of State) were to be seen in Glasgow Streets talking to ordinary people and, when Press-snappers were around, even shaking pensioners' hands and patting children's damp heads. Also to be seen abroad were House Factors and sun-tanned Property Owners who scurried around asking directions to the whereabouts of their life-support systems. Once the damage to their property had been assessed these Owners withdrew to such grey places as Miami or the Solomon Islands from where it was possible to take a more objective view of the catastrophe.

Meanwhile, Joe Public, his morale stiffened, his roof tarpaulined, quietly went on emptying his morning rain-bucket, confident that the authorities were doing all they could to promote his welfare. He could scarcely have been chuffed though if he chanced upon the following letter which appeared in a Glasgow newspaper at that post-storm time:

"Dear Editor,

Viewed from the flagpole at Queens Park, how picturesque – positively Parisian, in fact – the city looks with its gaily chequered rooftops. What a pity we shall, sooner or later, return to drab old slates..." It goes without saying that if the Glasgow Bucketeers had got their hands on this whimsical Francophile then the pole at Queens Park would have been burdened by something more apposite than a flag.

Although Joe Public was not to know it then, this letter with its sheen of smug self-interest, carried with it a presentiment of the rape of things to come when, only a couple of decades later, he would find himself betrayed by the Establishment of his grey and gallus city, find, too, that he was no longer welcome at the heart of it. In those days to come, when trees would outrank men, a tribe of mercenaries would occupy the centre of things, bumptious bipeds the Media would call Yuppies, a species of money-lice which would issue from the cracks in our fractured democracy.

But in his civic nest at George Square, Mother Kelly, that hatcher of media-speckled eggs, could be forgiven for underestimating the destabilizing consequences of the Administration's cow-towing and pandering to the Yuppies' avaricious needs. Beneath his wing at that time was an imposing clutch of projects that when hatched would earn him the reputation of having been the most entrepreneurial Provost ever to have graced his office. These projects included such sprightly chicks as the Burrell Collection, the GEAR Project, the Scottish Exhibition and Conference Centre, Glasgow's New Image campaign with its ludicrous logo about the city's claim – despite rotten back teeth and false front ones – to be able to outsmirk everyone else. Yes, he was Mr. Happy all right. But he was also a little puzzled. There was an odd egg in the batch – nicotine brown in colour. What on earth would hatch from it? So entranced had he become by this alien egg and its problematic contents that Mother Kelly seemed not to notice that there were a lot of Mr. Unhappy's parading before his Chambers' doors. Ironically, it seemed, he had been beguiled by his own slogan. If Glasgow was really miles better at anything then it must be at self-deception. For a start, what was miles better about the housing conditions in the Inner City and on the Urban Rim? In some pockets of squalor up to 35 per cent of the housing stock failed to meet the legal minima. It was estimated last year that something like a billion pounds would be required to effect repairs on up to 80,000 sub-standard homes throughout the city. We were miles better at producing truly shocking unemployment statistics too. Last year in the

Anderston ward, for instance, 45 per cent of those under 24 were without work. In July of that year in Woodlands the total stood at 57.79 per cent.

Civic crowing about a new Glasgow which was rising powerfully from the debris left by the collapse of the traditional chimney stack industries made a mockery of the privations being endured by those in the peripheral schemes like the Drum, Castlemilk and Easterhouse where those forerunners of social collapse – apathy and resignation – were to be seen with growing frequency. While the City Fathers were busy persuading themselves that 'the Bird that never flew' was in fact a phoenix that would rise to signal the birth of the Service Sector Renaissance, Mrs. Unhappy was on the lookout for something more mundane, perhaps a joiner, plasterers, or plumber who would do something to avert the collapse of her crumbling household. It would be of no comfort to her at all that once she was under the auspices of the new Housing Agency – Scottish Homes – she would be able to select her own landlord. This is tantamount to being told that although they are still going to hang you the choice of executioner is yours.

It was surely obvious from the start that the provision of executive flats in the Merchant City, the wholesale conversion of derelict warehouses, factories and lofts into yup-market homes would inaugurate obnoxious 'zones of exclusion' consequences, or, in street parlance, 'no-dough-no-go' areas, Yuppiedoms in fact, ghettos for the greedy, customised to cater for its inhabitants' taste for the good life. There would be, of course, no official, declaration of such a divisive policy but astronomical housing costs, and the inflated consumer goods prices would in the long run prove more effective gates or watchdogs at keeping 'the great unwashed' at bay. The working class citizen would be made to feel intimidated in this world of wynds, mews and shopping malls. The Briggait Market, for instance, with its toffee-nosed ambience is but a fore-runner of the snob-shops to come. Up in Buchanan Street, which is to be the focal point of the Glasgow Renaissance, the Princes Square development is knee-deep in ambience. All very ornate, yes, a cathedral dedicated to consumerism, imbued with the holy hush of money where the goods on offer are so pricey even the cheapest of them should carry a government wealth warning.

By now, of course, the city council, the SDA and the GA (Glasgow Action, a group of prominent business men) had got into their entrepreneurial stride. With their hands on their wallets GA pledged itself to assist in the economical and environmental regeneration of the city. It is well to remember, that some business men tend to think that the real Glasgow extends no further than Mother Kelly's well-scrubbed doorstep, i.e. Merchant City and Environs. The tacky bits, those beyond the pale like the inner city dole-traps and the ruination on the rim, well, these again in the street sense of the expression, have been well and truly scrubbed.

It is no surprise that a group like GA, whose chief aim is a 'dynamic and cosmopolitan city centre' should advocate a strategy of civic implosion, i.e.

energy flowing from rim to core, a centripetal force, and the direct opposite, in fact, to that centrifugal explosion triggered back in the Sixties by those poliscidal maniacs who called themselves Planners. The trashing of half the city in the name of 'slum clearance' was like the Dresden bombing – an unforgiveable act of community overkill.

Is this to be remedied, then? Is St. Mungo, with open arms, now calling his scattered children home? Yes, he is, but there are a few provisos: don't bother to come unless you are equipped with a blankety-blank chequebook and pen. Very expensive place to work, live and play in is Yuppieland. It's this ambience stuff, of course – it has to be specially imported. Another thing, don't bother to come if you are not young, adventurous, and willing to display shirt-sleeved heroism at the frontiers of Finance, or to demonstrate business courage above and beyond the call of lucre.

While, as befits an implosive strategy, the city's commercial core will draw upon its indigenous skill-banks to power the needs of the Service Sector Renaissance, it is acknowledged that there will have to be imported expertise. Financial planners, corporate lawyers, accountants, computer software personnel, etc. Such people will be in high demand as the city changes its economic pattern from a branch-office enterprise to one that will be sufficiently robust and expansive enough to attract and support corporate headquarters. This huge operation would perhaps not create a jobs bonanza but it would most certainlt cause an upsurge in vacancies for domestics, hotel staff, shop assistants, barmen, waitresses, security men, etc., though, as is the trend nowadays, much of this employment would be on a part-time basis.

Ten or so years ago it was difficult to persuade tourists that Glasgow was more than a grey launch-pad from which one took off to sample the delights of the real Scotland. This attitude has changed dramatically as the city has geared itself, both by an acceleration of hotel building and the creation of places of interest within Glasgow itself, to the promotion of a major tourist boom. The renovations and innovations taking place at present in the Merchant City itself is spearheading this tourist operation. Already in situ is the Tron Theatre, and a short distance from this is to be found the Briggait Market where lonely stallholders can be seen tossing herrings to catch a sprat. On now to St Enoch Square where there will be so much overhead glass they should have called it Pilkingtons Place. When this canopy is completed it is believed Glasgow will have the largest Starling Conference Centre in the world. It is the planners' intention to create a mini-village in this location where its higgledy-piggledy squares, wynds, and crooked passageways will be lit by the soft lantern-like glow of quaint shoppes and arty boutiques. Muggers? No, muggers are not to be allowed. Definitely not! Still under glass we cross from St Enochs into Buchanan Street were the opulent lure of Princes Square proves difficult to resist. But, since we are rather low in gold ingots we will proceed past it to where Gordon Square will be in the future with its exciting mixture of pavement cafes, restaurants, casinos – it will be quite Parisian, in fact.

No longer is the Clyde going to be allowed to slouch through the city like an old grey tramp – soon it is going to have work for its passage. Close by Kingston Bridge plans are being studied for the provision of a weir. This will, of course, eliminate tidal problems and it is hoped that floating restaurants can be moored here; accommodation for river craft will be provided, too, which could mean a place for the Waverley – if they can find out what keeps making it stop. There are big plans afoot for the adjacent Broomielaw – shops, bars, luxury homes – these will transform it into a desirable city location.

This year, of course, marks the city's Garden Festival. If the prices for admission to it prove to be accurate then no doubt it will come to be known as – 'The Dear Green Place'. Also this year the city will be host to the Baptist Youth Conference – an event which will accommodate some 10,000 delegates and will pump an estimated £4 million into the local economy. Another unusual event will be the Orchid Conference which is pencilled in for 1993. Glasgow and orchids might seem a strange mix but it is just another indication of the city's change of image. Maybe they will name one of the exotic blooms 'The Wee Hard Man' as a reminder of the infamous past.

1990, of course, is a year writ large in the Civic Diary – the year when Glasgow becomes a City of Culture. What an honour! Perhaps they will even throw an official Barmecide feast and invite all the no-jobbers and no-hopers to attend. Pardon? Call yourself cultured and you don't know what a Barmecide feast is! Of course you know, brother – you've been at such a feast ever since this Glasgow's Miles Better fantasy began. Yes, now you remember. That's it – a Barmecide feast is one where all the dishes are empty, an imaginary banquet. It came, as you say, from an Arabian Nights tale, the one in which the Barmecide prince gives the starving Schacabac such a feast for a jest. The ravenous man pretends to eat and relish the empty dishes set before him. But after he has consumed copious draughts of illusionary wine he feigns drunkeness and assaults the prince. The latter, seeing the humourous side, forgives Schacabac and provides him with food to his heart's content.

A cautionary tale perhaps for super-optimistic City Fathers and Yuppies imbued with an overweened sense of their own importance. The moral? Well, things might not work so amicably as in the story, for this time Schacabac will not be coming to the feast. Out there on the Urban Rim he will watch and bide his time. His brother will watch too from his Inner City wilderness. Both have had enough of feasting from empty plates and from equally empty promises. It would be wise to remember that a City which can work the miracle of changing violence into orchids also knows how to reverse the process.

A 15 year old's view of Glasgow from 'Geezabreak' by Colin Johnston, 1977.

JACK WITHERS

Glasgow Winter

There are only rare opinions
Scraping up bread for those walking dead

    Streaming walls and rain-washed visions
    Some no-go zones where they go slow and are afraid

Incomplete littered concrete
    Ghosts of clanking trams
Fleet of foot along dog-shit street
    Down-and-outs Tims and Jims

Oor Joe's bought a motor-car
Five hundred down then irregular payment

    Escalators of fear in every skyscraper
    Or a doom-room without shower in a wet-rot basement

Roars come from the hate-filled stadium
    Junkies get fixed on their sets
A rim of scum around a modern slum
    Alkies grope for blind dates

    The all-clear sounds in the soft stoned city
    Only pop and pot pollute the air
    Their destiny not harmony but social security
    Ear-plugged zombies sail past with unseeing stare

Their hair is mock Indian and blue
    Minds pure butter and chatter
Frozen emotion but not fashion on rivers of spew
    Unaware of future disaster

    And manipulated not educated
    An early broken crew
    Feelings all blasted and mutilated

WORKERS CITY

Few enquiring just who's kidding who

And they're living it up in the housing-schemes
    Suppressing their damned-up screams
And they're killing themselves in the pantomimes
    As bombs tick away in their dreams

    Mormons and morons and landlords of few words
    And no more ship's moans from a lifeless Clyde

On sweat-soaked beds lie demoralized reds
Swallowing vomit and thoughts of suicide

    So keep off the grass
    And don't pick up speed or pray for snow
    For there's nowhere then to go in big-time Glasgow

You could plunge in the syringe and forget about change
And join that same old line down at the labour exchange

GLESGA

GLESGA'S LITTER'S BETTER
GLESGA'S PURE WATTER
GLESGA SMELLS BITTER

GLESGA'S MYTHS TOTTER
GLESGA'S CHOOKIES CHATTER
GLESGA'S SLUMS SICKER
GLESGA'S CROAKS NATTER

GLESGA HEY MISTER
GLESGA SWILLS BETTER

GLESGA'S ARTISTS TITTER
GLESGA'S DOPE PUSHERS
GLESGA'S CITY FAITHERS

GLESGA'S WAN UPPERS
GLESGA'S NAE HOPERS
GLESGA'S COMIC OPERAS
GLESGA'S KIDDER OANERS

GLESGA'S MINDLESS MUGGERS
GLESGA'S AIN GOALERS

GLESGA'S DOPE FIXERS
GLESGA'S MALES BATTER
GLESGA'S INCHOATE STUTTER

GLESGA'S LAIDBACK LOSERS
GLESGA MAYFEST DISASTER
GLESGA'S PATTER'S WATTER
GLESGA'S HOLY ROLLERS

GLESGA AH LOVE HER

Dear Grey City

Huv ye heard o' St. Mungo and the fish, the tree and the bell
And the Gorbals and Strathbungo or the auld Bar-L?
Well, the city is Glesga renowned faur and wide
For its slogans oan the wa's and great queens o' the Clyde

Its buildings ur high its expectancies low
'Cause thir's damp in the banes o' auld Glasgow
That's compared wi' Chicago yon hell-hole o' crime
Big jungle ca'd Glesga playin for time

Aye and the Indians huv come in wan helluva hurry
Japattis and papadoms an burnin hot curry
An thir's Micks an Sikhs and bhoys in royal blue
Beastin it like slaves or rottin oan the burroo

O dear grey city they luv tae ca' green
Never sae pretty as when it is mean
That exists wi' a myth o' humour an hert
Stale pooder oan the face o' a blowsy auld tart

An then thir wis planners wha' tore doon the slums
An spewed up new hames but failt in thir sums
Aye an the provost cin dance an swing oan his chain
While the minds o' the folk pours doon the drain

For thir's big-time sharks and penthoose-rats
Cowcaddens cowboys an fat west-end cats
Wee sly dope-pushers an fly con-men
O wull the Clyde ever be deep red again?

Somewhere between St. George's Cross and Hillhead Underground

Ur ye sure we're oan the right line? In which direction ur we moving?

Dead straight, though bent. Like light. Curved, eventually circular. Darling round and round we go, round and round we go...

Always the same it is, nothin chynges. Fed-up wi' it ah um.

Too bad. There's no escape.

Nae optin-oot?

Opting out? Where to? To an unnattainable Eden in our great cultured town? Paradise is lost, honey, lost. Long since. O serpent, serpent in damp basement, slither on to full enlightenment.

Sometimes ah wonder aboot you so ah dae.

Good. For without wonder we're lost.

It stinks down here.

And up there.

And naebdy talks tae ye or even luks at ye.

Everybody an island. A wee Barlinnie.

Surrounded by litter.

O this our proud and native midden where everything's open and nothing's hidden.

Whit a come-doon – skyscraper tae underground, an headin naewhere. Ye'd think thir wis a war oan or sumthin.

There's always a war on. Peace-time is a misnomer. We can't manage it for we're constantly at war with each other – and ourselves. Only great maturity and insight brings a kind of peace. And that has to be worked for real hard.

If thir's anither yin it'll be the last yin, that's for sure. A war.

Uneasy in peace, always preparing, we never learn.

Ah learnt early tae take it oan the chin and still grin.

Is that the reason?

Whit dae ye mean?

Is that the reason why the world's insane? O insanity, insanity, or do we mean humanity?

Ssshhh.

Ssshhh? Why should I?

Cause folk ur lukin at us.

Who cares? Let them. They might learn something that would help bring them out of their own narrow and inhibited little selves.

Like what?

Like thinking. Like taking an interest in the wider community. Like refusing to be exploited and manipulated. Like working on self-discipline. Like learning to eliminate that corrosive fear that steadily eats away at our distant and instinctive heritage of folk wisdom and roots. Like not being so spineless, passive and clueless. Like refusing to be divided. Like asking who, what, where, when, why.

Keep yir voice doon for god's sake.

Why should I when I'm only beginning to find it?

Cause people ur no used tae it. They luk up and keek and then luk away again. Deid embarrassed they ur. Deid embarrassed.

Except for that secret policeman taking notes in the corner seat.

Secret policeman? O come on. This is Glesga – European culchural city an a' that, no Moscow. We don't have secret polis in this toon. Run o' the mill cops, sure, but secret wans. We're deid democratic an that.

That's comforting to know.

Is it? Good.

Glasgow. Great social security city. New Jerusalem of the north. Gleaming cultural jewel. Tiara for Tamara. Forget about debt and borrow for tomorrow. Have a ball in seasons of fine hel.. Chekhov and piss-off. Blue socks in Ibrox. Bolshoi Ballet in the Dennistoun Palais. Pablo Casals doon in the Gorbals. O there' Berlin and Athens and Paris, and London and Venice and a', but if yese insist we'll tell ye whaur's best and it's no Bogota or Tokyo: for it's Glesga, it's Glesga, it's Glesga, dear auld Glesga toon, when yir oot oan the batter in Glesga then ye don't mind the acid rain...

Aw geezabrek wull ye? Whit's got intae ye ata', eh?

The truth. The whole truth and nothing but the truth. I've seen the light.

JANETTE McGINN

Gizza Hoose

IN APRIL AND May of 1983 the people of Castlemilk, passing on their way to the shops or to pay their rent, became accustomed to the sight of the three gaily-decorated caravans tucked neatly inside the grounds of the offices of the Glasgow District Council Housing Management Department. It was a good spell of weather and excitement was high. 'Sit-in' supporters patrolling the pathway alongside the caravans invited passers-by to sign their petition or make a small donation to the campaign by tossing whatever coppers they could afford into one of the bright plastic buckets which hung from the railings.

Inside the grounds, others busied themselves shaking out sleeping bags and blankets and hanging them on the railings, sweeping the steps of the caravans, lifting pieces of rubbish from the ground and when necessary feeding the two stray dogs who had attached themselves to the protesters. The smell of cooking from the caravans wafted in the air and the strains of music added to the feeling of excitement. Much good natured banter was exchanged and many tales recounted of experiences at the hands of the housing department.

During these weeks, the protesters patiently explained to those who stopped alongside why the caravans were there and outlined the events leading up to this strange situation.

On a Tuesday evening some weeks before, the three families who were the subject of the protest had been awakened from their sleep by some kind of explosion from the ground floor flat in the building where they stayed. This was quickly followed by a fire and when the Fire Brigade eventually rescued the families it was by turntable from the balconies of their homes. They had been given accommodation at Glasgow's Homeless Unit on a night to night basis, but eventually told that they would have to return to their homes the following Monday. The families were refusing to return. It was impossible, they said, to live in the houses in the condition they were in, but more importantly, they were convinced that the explosion had been caused by a petrol bomb being thrown into the ground floor flat. They were terrified of returning and insisting that they be rehoused. But housing officials had opposing priorities. In this 'difficult to let' area tenants had come and gone and close after close had been boarded up and remained unoccupied. The housing department now dug their heels in, determined that this particular close was not going to be added to their existing list. The houses were habitable, they insisted, and if a bomb had indeed been the cause of the explosion then thise was a matter for the police and had nothing to do with the housing authorities. Before the following Monday, a group of people had formed themselves in support of the tenants. The press and television had been contacted and photos had been taken of the 'habitable' houses. The local M.P. John Maxton had himself inspected the houses and had suffered breathing difficulties in the close and stairs without even entering the houses.

On the Monday, the tenants refused to move back into the houses and the Homeless Unit refused to give them further accommodation. On Tuesday the housing department did in fact respond by sending out the building and works who set to scrubbing down walls and stairs in an attempt to make the building habitable. Still the families refused to return and had their furniture removed and left with friends for safe-keeping. They themselves had to find accommodation from wherever they could. The group of supporters rapidly increased in number and harried councillors and housing officials without success. By the following week after a lengthy packed meeting in the Jeely Piece Resource Centre, a further course of action was agreed. The following day, the three families with friends and supporters, occupied the Castlemilk Office of the Housing Management Department and spent the day explaining to people why they wanted alternative housing and how this was being refused. At closing time those prepared to risk arrest remained in the office. This course of action continued for more than a week and each night the police were called in. Some nights, after being invited to leave by the police, the protesters would go, sometimes they wouldn't and sometimes they weren't given a choice but bundled into the police van. On one occasion the police arrived on foot, but unfortunately those arrested declined the invitation to walk the short distance to the local police station and a call had to be put out for the vans. Over a period of some eight days, 48 arrests were made, 12 people being arrested on four occasions. On the last occasion, the charge was 'Breach of the Peace' and as this was more serious than the previous charges of 'Trespass', court appearances were scheduled for 2 days later. The protesters made plans for a spectacular court appearance. Each of the 12 approached different lawyers, asking them to appear at court on their behalf. Posters and demonstrations outside the court were arranged and a Press Release was prepared. It was going to be an occasion! However on the evening before the court appearances, a policeman arrived at the offices of the Housing Department where he knew he would find the accused and produced letters for all informing them that their appearance the following day was no longer required. Nothing further was ever heard from the police regarding the 48 arrests they had made!

By this time however, tactics had changed and the next plan of action – the erection of tents, replaced a day later by donated caravans – quickly followed.

So, now after a couple of weeks, people had grown used to the sight of the three caravans in the grounds of the Housing Department. Most people were now aware that each caravan symbolised the shelter which the families had

Phil Goldie and 'Pops' at the Castlemilk Sit-In.

chosen rather than return to their previous homes.

Posters caricaturing the recently appointed Director of Housing, Paul Mugnaioni, and reading 'Wanted Mugsy Baloney, May be Posing as Housing Director' were pasted all over the caravans. A slogan from a TV series was adapted and 'Castlemilk Sit-In' posters and lapel badges with 'C'mon, Gizza Hoose' were everywhere.

The protesters drew up a roster of volunteers for day and night duty, but the caravans were always full of people. Sleeping bags, blankets, food, cutlery were to hand and no-one was ever hungry or cold. Groups came along to entertain the 'Sit-In'; local shops donated foodstuffs and some three weeks into the campaign a supporters dance was held. Still the Housing Department continued to argue that it was all a matter for the police and nothing to do with them. Still the caravans remained in the grounds and nobody attempted to move them or the people living in them.

Group meetings continued to be held daily, a visit to Mugnaioni was made and while all were aware the situation was causing headaches in political circles, it seemed that neither the Councillors, the Housing Department or the Director of Housing were going to be shamed into re-housing the families and continued to insist it was a police matter. Rumours were in fact about that the Police Special Patrol Group were patrolling the area at night.

However like any good, well-organised campaign, more than one avenue was being pursued and so alongside the Gizza Hoose Sit-In, negotiations were going on with the Housing Management for re-housing, using medical grounds and similar tactics which allowed them to back down gracefully and so some six weeks after the fire, the three families had satisfactory offers of re-housing and victory was achieved. The six houses in the closes the tenants had come from remained unoccupied, was boarded up and a security guard posted in the area. The sit-in caravan occupation of the Housing Department had lasted almost four weeks.

Five years later many questions remain unanswered. Why the clamp down on publicity? At the beginning of the campaign while the protest was still fairly tame and no doubt following similar line to the respectable and acceptable community work exercise of petitions, posters, haranging the councillors, and the occasional orderly demonstration, the press and TV appeared really interested and used the material given. But once the tempo quickened and it became clear clear that this was not an easily controllable group following a community worker paid by the Council, but a real gut protest from able individuals of varying political persuasions of the left and many ordinary angry people prepared to take a stand against injustice, the media cooled off and while for a time reporters and photographers continued to arrive and were very interested, this did not find its way to the newspapers. Did the media really lose interest?

Why were the charges against those arrested dropped and the court appearances cancelled? Who made these decisions? Why were they made? It would seem that having the charges dropped required the agreement of the District Council, the Regional Council, the Police and the Courts. Was the establishment afraid that if word got about, caravans would be moved into similar sites in other housing schemes in Glasgow and perhaps the people in Easterhouse, Drumchapel or Pollok would also say "We prefer to live in an old caravan rather than accept the conditions you are forcing upon us!"

Or maybe indeed the wall of silence which surrounded Castlemilk and the unique happenings there had something to do with the embarrassing fact that the then Lord Provost Michael Kelly had just launched his much acclaimed 'Glasgow's Miles Better' campaign. It was perhaps unfortunate that this coincided with Castlemilk's 'Gizza Hoose' Sit-In, but one thing is certain: none of the photographs taken of the latter found their way into Dr. Kelly's campaign publicity brochures!

Cartoons by Rab Paterson from 'Castlemilk Today'.

FARQUHAR McLAY

Playboys

NOTE: For many years Lord Provost McTinn of Glasgow travelled the globe from one great capital to another. It was long rumoured that throughout his travels he kept a journal in which was recorded, in minute and sometimes disturbing detail, his most intimate experiences with important and powerful leaders of the world. The journal is believed to have comprised some two dozen 120-sheet Big Value Jotters which, we now know, had been gifted to him by the SCWS from their now defunct Stationery Department at 398 Paisley Road, Glasgow, on the eve of his departure for Ottawa. As well as brief day-to-day entries the journal contained longer and more finished passages, whole chapters of autobiography, in fact, which were clearly intended for the public, either in the form of published memoirs, or lectures, or, maybe, after-dinner speeches. Sadly all two dozen books of the journal disappeared following a mysterious burglary at McTinn's home shortly after his return from Jidda. Although gold and silver swords, an Arabian jewelled dagger and other gifts and valuables said to be worth well in excess of £900,000 were on the premises at the time and ready to hand, only the notebooks were taken. To this day the thief's identity remains unknown. His, or indeed her, purpose in wishing to lay hands on this substantial historical document, has been variously conjectured. If, however, suppression was the object it has signally failed. Extracts purporting to be from McTinn's journal, some of extremely doubtful authenticity, let it be said, have popped up in the Far East, the Middle East and the Near East, in the Mid West, the North West and the Far North, as well as in the Deep South and, more recently, on the South Side. Many of these unauthenticated texts are mere crude pornography. For example in the Port Said edition the Prince of Mecca flagellates McTinn with a sjambok. And again, in an account emanating from Milan (M XXI ms.7) McTinn, in the nude, plays the organ in the Papal Chapel while the Pope flagellates himself. The fragment published here is the Mecca version (Z IV ms.1) which has been scrupulously collated with all other verifiable editions. In the absence of internal evidence to the contrary, and with no better data to go on, I think we can safely accept this as being as close to McTinn's original text as we are ever likely to get.

*   *   *

THE SAUDI PRINCE was full of breeding, with a royal dignity of head and shoulders. Such was his colossal stature that one could only marvel at the manner in which he put up with our trade delegation – such pygmies we must have seemed to him.

But by rights I ought to begin with the Mayor of Jidda, a tall, graceful, vigorous man with whom I at once struck up a terrific bond of friendship. He played backgammon with my wife in the guest tent and was fond of reciting lengthy passages from the Koran, the whole of which he had committed to memory in boyhood. It was through the Mayor of Jidda that my Arabian adventure really got underway.

One morning he had me kitted out in the regalia of Sherif Fauzan ibn Tikheim his bosom friend, with ceremonial dagger and all. The hilt of that dagger was studded with priceless jewels, and it was only with the greatest reluctance, not wishing to offend, yet fearful I might lose it, that I was persuaded to carry it about my person. They packed me off, with a specially padded saddle under me, on Biseita, the Mayor's favourite she-camel, to ride the lonely velvet sands of the Wad Murrmiya.

Bedouin tribesmen bowed their heads as I passed. The Bedouin, let me tell you are a hard and pitiless race. They are wholly imbued with the spirit of the desert harsh and repellent, and cannot act otherwise but in accordance with that spirit. Their chief delight would seem to be directing strangers to wells which they know to be dry, and even to wells which do not in fact exist and have never existed. To succour the afflicted seems to the Bedouin a monstrous aberration: their natural disposition is to finish you off and take your belongings. Yet how different, how very different, it proved to be in my case!

When I lost control of Biseita in the Wadi Fura and was pitched headlong into the sand, I thought my hour had come. The carrion crows hovered above me and resigned myself to death in the wilderness, far from family and friends.

And as I composed myself for the final ordeal my whole career passed before my eyes as in some wondrous vision. With the hand of death clutching at my throat, it was that vision alone which eased my spirit and sustained me. All things were suddenly made crystal clear. Yes I had made mistakes, and they were not hidden from me, but my successes far outweighed them. In the scale of eternal values would be vindicated. My decision to become the roving ambassador for our fair city had been the correct one. That above all was what cheered and comforted me and enabled me to endure. I had chosen the right course rather than the easy one. I had kept faith with destiny. In my terrible anguish that vision consoled me. I knew my pre-ordained task would be fulfilled.

Those who scoffed when I resisted their urgings to confine my duties to a narrow sphere – they would be cast down. And the mud-slingers who said I was taking long holidays at the ratepayers' expense, and free-wheeling round the world simply to amass a personal fortune out of gifts received from high dignitaries in Rome, Milan

Ottowa, London, Warsaw, Kabul, Mecca, Medina, Jidda, Peking, Shanghai, Canton and all along the Great Wall of China – these detractors would be scattered and confounded and put to shame.

My mission was to salvage and restore the broken and blighted image of our town. Consider the disrepute into which we had fallen before I began my travels. Even the Bedouin bandit who came to my rescue in a red Toyota truck – yes even he, Abd el Shimt Bataab, porn merchant, even he had heard of us. He even believed we must be descended from a tribe of professional robbers of pilgrims – a tribe banished in ancient times by a false Emir and blood-brothers to the Bedouin. It was due entirely to this mythical Arab connection that my life was spared. (Not that it saved Sherif Fauzan's jewelled dagger, signed by Mufaddhi, the greatest swordsmith in all Arabia; it was stolen from me as I slept, after a feast in my honour at a watering-place called Abu Markha.)

On arrival back in Jidda a most fantastic reception awaited me. Scenes of wild delirium all around. Wherever I stopped a sumptuous banquet was immediately prepared.

The story of my desert travail had gone before me. Without in any way desiring it, and indeed completely unknown to me, I had become a hero and celebrity overnight. Everywhere I went people kept rushing up to me with tears in their eyes and showering me with gifts of money and victual. "No!" I yelled, "I am not the Prophet!". But my words were drowned in their tumultuous acclaim.

As we neared the centre of the town the crowds grew even larger and soon there were tens of thousands flocking round me. The Prince's soldiery had to fend them off with whips. But the more bloodily the soldiers lashed out, the more fervent these zealots became. At length some live ammunition was distributed among the troops, and I was whisked away to the Royal Palace. There I was reunited with my dear wife. It seems she had abandoned all hope of ever seeing me again, and such was the shock occasioned by my sudden appearance before her, that she fell away in a swoon. My friend and colleague Bashir Kahn, who was part of the delegation, openly wept. The Mayor of Jidda, alas, was absent from the gathering: I learnt later he had been called out urgently to help quell the rioting. Indeed intermittent bursts of machine-gun fire could be heard during the whole of that never-to-be-forgotten night.

Somewhere in the courtyard, Abdul Pasha, ancient laureate of the Saudis, intoned his First and Second Hymn to the Prophet. This bold work was composed in the first instance to commemorate the arrival of our trade mission. It was now greatly expanded to take in the whole of my desert adventure and triumphal return to Jidda.

Princess Mieff, a most gifted lady, graciously undertook to render the whole of this very long poem into English. You can imagine how deeply affected I was. But judge of my feelings when she bent down and whispered that at any moment now I was to have bestowed upon me the highest honour in all Arabia. My head was spinning.

I could not think what was happening to me as I was led away, dazed an
bewildered, down long meandering corridors and up huge flights of steps. I caugh
a glimpse of Bashir deep in business negotiations with some sheiks. I noticed to
that my dear wife seemed not yet to have recovered from her little upset and wa
sprawled out on the floor of the courtyard with nobody paying the least attentior
At last we stopped at a massive gateway which looked to be constructed out of soli
gold. And I realised at once what was happening: I had been summoned to th
Royal Presence.

The Prince was striding towards me, the last word in breeding, a royal dignity c
head and shoulders.

"I want you to tell me everything" said the Prince, taking me by the elbow an
ushering me to a couch. "You must leave out not a single detail. So far I have hear
rumours merely. If half of what I have heard is true, you may rest assured we shal
not be displeased."

I did as the Prince bade me and left nothing out. By degress I came to the par
about my wondrous vision in the desert when I was exalted and saw myself elect and
justified in all my transactions and decisions, both public and private. I recounted
every little thing I could remember, exactly as it had occurred, withou
embellishment or deletion. Finally I told of my deliverance at the hands of the porr
bandit Abd el Shimt Bataab who, on discovering the name of my native place
hailed me as a brother of the true blood, one of a lost tribe of the Bedu, and had me
escorted safely back to Jidda amidst unheard of and amazing scenes of mad joy
During the whole of my narration the Prince sat very close to me on the divan and
from time to time placed a hand on my knee and in a low, croaking kind of voice
kept saying something like "It is the will of Allah, it is the will of Allah", to which
thought it prudent simply to nod my head and go on with the story.

When I had finished, the Prince took several long, deep inhalations of air and
threw himself back amongst the silken cushions. He lay with his back to me for a
long time. I could not think what was expected of me. I had heard stories of hi
delicate health.

I was beginning to wonder whether the Prince had had a seizure, an epileptic fit
perhaps, for his body jerked about violently for some minutes in a most disquieting
manner, and then his whole frame seemed to be convulsed, and I was in something
of a quandary as to whether I should summon help.

Then, as suddenly as it had overtaken him, whatever it was, it was gone, and I
found the Prince staring up at me with cold, almost malevolent eyes, as if he held me
in some way responsible for what had happened.

Without a word he sprang from the divan, pulled his robes around him, lit a
cigarette, and began to pace restlessly up and down.

"I must humbly beg your Royal Highnesses's pardon" I said, "if anything I have
done or any word I have uttered has been offensive to you."

I bowed my head very low and slid onto one knee. There was a long time during which my head remained sunk low. The Prince came round to where I was kneeling and stood over me. I could feel he was to some extent mollified now, seeing me in that respectful posture.

"The Golden Sword of Mecca" said the Prince, "is never lightly bestowed, nor is the Silver Sword of Jidda granted to the unworthy."

"I am at your feet, your Royal Highness" I said. "Show me in what way I may prove myself worthy, for I know not, being a stranger in your beautiful country, and I fear I may have erred unwittingly or in some way caused offence without intending anything of the kind."

"This Abd el Shimt Bataab" said the Prince, "he is well known to us. A purveyor of shameless and dissolute filth, a pernicious renegade and transgressor of Shariah law. He has been condemned by the Wahhabi, which means you are not permitted to sleep with him, eat with him, converse with him or give countenance to any communication regarding him which is not couched in terms of the most bitter disparagement."

The Prince was up so close to me that the folds of his gamboz, which he wore with superb style and dignity, ruffled the hair on my bowed head, and I became aware of a most delightful aroma enveloping me as I knelt there on his silken olive-green carpet.

"He has crossed and re-crossed the desert many times" the Prince went on, "from the mountain fastnesses of Taif to Dhahran, to Jidda, to Riyadh and even to Mecca itself, with his caravan of red Toyota trucks which contain filthy videos. I suppose you lay in his private tent? I suppose he regaled you with some films?"

I gave my head two quick little shakes, not looking up, to signify total and unreserved denial.

"There are other considerations, of course" the Prince continued. "By the code of Hammurabi the trafficking in such merchandise condemns him. But there is more. Abd el Shimt Bataab is a nomadic pastoralist who preaches against oil and settled agriculture. Wherever he appears there are disturbances and people leave their little wooden huts and once again take to the camel and the tent and go roaming the desert to evade the tax!"

Yet again I shook my head rapidly two or three times, and I gasped, and I squirmed, hoping by all this to convey to the Prince my sense of shock and outrage.

"It's all right" said the Prince. "My Chief of Police, Gasim Fuad Bey, is hot on his trail. Abd el Shimt Bataab's reign of savagery is near to its close. What concerns me more —" and here the Prince raised my head in both his hands and stared penetratingly into my eyes – "is you! This blood-brother connection you speak of. That's what worries me. It may be nonsense of course. And yet – from what I've heard of your town and townspeople... If you are of the banished tribe of the Bedu, a tainted race, you are by nature rebellious. The high ideals of wealth and luxury, grace, breeding, culture, leave you cold. The very concept of authority and power

and the law makes you boke. I could not in all honesty advise anyone to inves
money in your schemes. It would be nothing but aggravation."

My mind was racing. Clearly our rivals had stolen a march on us. Flagran
untruths had been disseminated among the sheiks. The good name of our city ha
been dragged through the dirt. We had been depicted as anarchists an
revolutionaries out to shatter the very fabric of the State itself. These absur
calumnies had obviously reached the ears of the Prince. How was I, a long-standin
member of the Labour Party, to convince his Highness of the sheer bliss I wa
experiencing, and the thousand and ones sensations of voluptuous joy whic
coursed through me, as I knelt there on his silken olive-green carpet?

After a hasty invocation to the Virgin Mother of Good Counsel, that she migh
lead me to say and do all the right things at that critical juncture, I began in thi
wise:

"Your Royal Highness, may I be permitted to attempt to rectify what I very muc
fear has been a gross misrepresentation of the true character and natura
disposition of my people? You surely know that there are unprincipled types goin
about, who, for their own ends and objects, would like to see us vilified an
muddied in your gracious Majesty's esteem. No doubt they have tried to portray u
as a gang of footpads and firebrands. But let me assure you the truth is ver
different. In all my travels it has seldom been my good fortune to meet wit
anything to equal the unique supineness of our national character. The nearest I go
to it was among the Dahomeans on the Guinea Coast and in certain of the Witot
clans of North Western Amazonia. We are an abject people, my Prince, utterl
craven and base, emasculated of all spirit and made tractable and stupid on
massive scale. Our jails are hell-holes –"

"Ah!" interposed the Prince. "I see a contradiction here. I am told your jails ar
overflowing. How is it, if your people are so docile, they have to be locked away i
such large numbers?"

"Because" I replied, the truth blowing into my mind like the Gift of Tongue
"life on the outside is just as bad. Our wretched discards no longer care very muc
one way or the other. DHSS poverty kills. Those who do not actually perish in th
flesh will, most infallibly and in due time, perish in spirit. Unlike your Benignan
Royal Highness, we do not just chop limbs – we butcher the soul!"

"Sorcery?" inquired the Prince.

"Education" I replied. "Compulsory education. It is very important. You hav
to catch them young, if you see what I mean."

"You have specialists in that work?"

"We do, we do. They are absolutely indispensable. We manufacture them in ou
schools and universities. Afterwards they go into the community and take jobs i
the media or public relations or teaching or medicine or politics or art or anythin
you care to mention and go right on furthering the good work: dealing death to th
human spirit and freeing us forever from the pernicious frivolity of revolt. Yo

could take the Labour Party as a pretty good example of what I mean. Or Jimmy Reid. Or Margo MacDonald. You never saw two like that for sinking the human spirit. In drama, in literature, in art they abound, keeping the people meek, keeping the world safe for authority."

"Yet for all that" said the Prince, fondling my hair, "some not so meek slip through. This John MacLean I've been hearing about. Maybe not an Abd el Shimt Bataab, but very dangerous nonetheless. How can I be sure there are not others just like him waiting to pounce? How can I be sure your people are not more cunning than abject?"

"I'm glad you brought that up" I put in quickly. "That little episode in our history only serves to illustrate my point more forcibly. When the rebel was convicted and sent to the hell-hole, the mob, if you recall, followed him to the gates of that place in their tens of thousands. And when the gates of the hell-hole were slammed behind their hero, what did the mob do? I'll you, my Lord Prince. They scuttled off home to get their tea, in their tens of thousands, and left their hero there to rot. They just slunk off home, quietly and orderly, like the good citizens they were – back to the peeces of bread and lard, back to a khaki uniform or a bench in the munitions factory, back to redeem the alarm clocks MacLean had urged them to pawn, back to the TB and the rickets and the highest infant mortality rate this side of Calcutta!"

"Incredible" said the Prince.

"Not in the least" I went on. "Nothing could have been more natural. None of this was any hardship to them. It was MacLean that was their hardship, and we had relieved them of that. We had given them back what they most desired in their heart of hearts: the right to grovel. Now they could return, with an easy conscience, to their old obsequious ways: for to duck and bob and bow and scrape was all their love. We even took their space and cleared them out to ghettoes at the far perimeter: we ordered them out and they went, like frightened sheep, so that developers could make a bundle. What fervour of subservience was there!"

"In such an uncouth race" mused the Prince, "I'd have expected bombs."

"Bombs!" I exlaimed, or rather spluttered, my head muffled in the Prince's costly robes. "Did you say bombs?"

"Yes" said the Prince airily, "bombs. Government buildings going up in smoke. Policemen stretched out dead in the street."

Such was the consternation engendered in me by these last remarks I was struck dumb. I suddenly drew back from him and felt myself trembling from top to toe as I knelt there. For a moment I thought I was about to vomit.

Then, in a wonderfully soothing voice, the Prince said: "It is nothing, my little friend. Nothing. What have we to fear? We are leaders of the world, but safe here in the Palace of the Prince."

(Perhaps I should advert here to the fact that, from this moment onwards the Prince used this mode of address when we were *en tete-a-tete* together, but somehow it managed to get out and very soon the fawning sheiks, who seethed with envy on account of my position of influence with his Royal Highness, and all the numerous Palace retainers, were referring to me as "the Prince's little friend" which pleased me mightily and endowed our trade mission with much glamour and prestige.)

"My dear Prince," I resumed, once I had collected myself, "you do our dear old proletariat a grievous wrong. The only blood they've ever spilt is their own."

"A neat solution" said the Prince.

"Very neat" I added quickly. "And what's more, you can rely on the Labour Party to keep it neat. That's what we're here for. We are against all forms of simplistic (that is to say direct and effective) action – especially when perpetrated for political or economic gain. We don't mind people protesting about dog shit on the pavement. That is perfectly proper and democratic. Canine control is a legitimate issue. To put it in a nutshell, your Royal Highness: We have the people by the balls! Just trust us. If Capitalism goes down the stank, the Labour Party goes with it. If privilege is swept away, how are we to get ourselves knighthoods and OBEs, amass fortunes, become landlords and send our children to private schools? It doesn't bear thinking about. All we ask is a little trust. Look at it this way: we, the Labour Party, speak for the people. What is the result? The people stay dumb. We act for the people: and the people stay impotent. We think for the people: and the people stay children. The system is fool-proof."

When I had said these things the Prince once again took my head in both his hands and drew me close to his person.

"You have spoken well" said the Prince, "and your words have pleased us. Henceforth we shall look kindly upon you and upon your mission. Your people have found favour in our eyes, and they shall be to us even as our own, for verily your people and my people have much in common."

At that moment I underwent a most beautiful experience. It was indeed as if all the cares of the world, and all the toilsome burdens of office, had been lifted clean off my shoulders. It was as if all the baffling perplexities of life were dissolved in that moment of languorous ease. A secret voluptuous tremor passed through me, and with it a feeling of the most intense, the most sublime gratification.

Kneeling there I bethought me of the Wanderer in Holy Scripture who, at his journey's end, exclaims: O yea, it is good to be here! I have travelled too long in strange lands. In a word, I found myself in a state of delirious contentment: as if I had eaten of the lotus flower and time and the world had faded from my ken and I and my Calypso were one!

O yea, I have wandered in deserts, and in mountains, and in dens and caves of the earth, and endured the unendurable for our fair city, but there were moments, and this was one of them, when the reward was of such magnitude as to make all my pains and travail seem as nothing.

I listened to the interminable drone of the good Abdul Pasha who was closetted nearby, on a stool, in the Prince's private elevator, as he intoned the First and Second Hymn to the Prophet.

All night the machine guns chattered away and one heard the odd shriek and cry of pain coming up from the street. Doubtless Abd el Shimt Bataab was now captured, and the chief of police, Gasim Fuad Bey, would be pouring the wealth of Arabia, in boiling little driblets, down the rebel's throat.

At that moment I was under a spell which nothing could break.

Towards morning two deaf and dumb eunuchs fetched us the cardamon-flavoured coffee in a brass pot with a long spout. The playful Prince lounged at his ease beside me, and with charming and astonishing *eclat* blew smoke rings into the air.

I fell to thinking of all I had come through to reach the citadel. The days and nights I battled through the simoom, the snake bite at the Wadi Itm, the fever, the thirst – and here at last my reward. I thought of the trust that had been placed in me by merchant bankers and high-grade entrepreneurs at home. And I was easy in the conscience, knowing I had faced my obligations in their totality and discharged my functions as Provost/Ambassador with zeal right to the end.

Suddenly the Prince took a powerful grip on my arm just above the elbow. "My little friend" he said, "let me prophesy. I see a time coming, and that time not far off, when your city will become one of the great capitals of the world. Business confidence will be restored and high finance will flourish. There will be huge redevelopments. I see sun-tanned men in cadillacs coming from the east and west to see wonders of high art and extravagant culture. And they will put money in your purse till your purse bulges and overflows. And you shall be a city of tycoons and whizz-kids and high rollers."

"That's it!" I shouted. "That's it! That's what we want!"

"But the dead ones" the Prince continued, "the ones you have thrust from your bosom, they shall be nowhere in sight. They shall neither see, nor touch, nor even smell this money. Nor shall they benefit from it in any way whatsoever, unless, perhaps, as the coolie benefits from the burden strapped to his back."

O yea, it is good to be here.

IAIN NICOLSON

I HAVE BEEN unable to find any biographical material relating to this poet. The song below (along with another called 'The South Down Milita') appeared in an undated publication, 'The Rebels Ceilidh Song Book', sometime, more than likely, in the mid 1950s. Any information regarding this author would be welcome.

The Provost in the song is Paddy Dollan (Sir Patrick Dollan, Lord Provost of Glasgow 1938-41) – a one-time radical from Baillieston who made a long and, one might suppose, lucrative career for himself in civic politics. He ended up with a string of chairmanships – East Kilbride Development Corporation, Advisory Council for Civil Aviation, Scottish Fuel Efficiency Committee – the first St Mungo prize (£1,000), probably invented with him in mind, and a knighthood. He died in 1963 untainted by any accusation of having failed tae luik oot for hesel.

'Old Barnhill' was the Poorhouse in the north of Glasgow, later renamed Foresthall.

The Labour Provost

Tune: The White Cockade

When I was young and fu' o' fire
Tae smash the Tories was my firm desire
But noo I'm auld I hae' mair sense
I just blame the lot on Providence.

Chorus:
　　I am a man o' high degree
　　Lord Provost o' this great cittee
　　The workers want a world tae gain
　　But I'm content wi' my badge and chain.

Wi' John Maclean and Willie Gallacher
Yince I thocht I micht ha'e travelled far
But noo the thocht, it fairly makes me pale
Wanst I landed in Barlinnie Jail!

Chorus

Wi' ma ermine coat and my office seal
For Socialism I am fu' o' zeal
The principles of socialism are a' very well
Bit ye mustnae forget tae look after yersel.

Chorus

Let the Russians bum aboot their five year plans
Their tractors, factories and Hydro dams
Lang afore thae Bolshies had an ounce o' skill
We up and nationalised old Barnhill.

Chorus

Lang afore the Poles or Rumanians
The Czechoslovaks or Bulgarians
We led the workers on tae victorie
We municipalised the Govan Ferree.

Chorus

So whan the Queen cam's tae see us a'
Republican sentiments we'll banish awa'
On bended knee, or if it suits,
On hunkers doon we'll lick her boots.

MATT McGINN
(1928-1977)

IT WOULD SURELY be an astonishing thing if bribery and corruption belonged exclusively to Westminster politics and the London Stock Exchange. As guide and ruler and example they point the way. The tail-end must simply follow where the head leads. If civic politics is nothing but cheapjack roguery you have to admit the blueprint was pretty crooked from the start. Councillor Inglis was by no means the first, and certainly he was not the last, civic luminary in Glasgow to be found to be heavily into crookery. A great many have been exposed over the years and, if form is anything to go by, it is quite likely a great many more will be exposed in the future. It is remarkable, though, how few people are really surprised whenever the veil is momentarily ripped apart and we are allowed to glimpse the extent of the cesspit within. As Matt McGinn suggests at the end of his song, the ex-senior magistrate might easily have had a good many civic dignataries for company in Peterhead.

A' for a Pub Hoose Licence

If you're oot o' luck in Glasgow I'll be having a word with you.
Don't go signing at the Labour Exchange, it isn't the thing to do.
Though they're not so very good at it they might give you a job.
No, just you come along with me and I'll fix you with a pub.

> *Chorus:*
> Now, the licence is the thing we want, but don't have any fears,
> There's a man I know will have a word in some o' the judges' ears.
> As long as your pockets jingle you can come along with me,
> We will speak tae Bailie Inglis, he's the very man tae see.

Now, Inglis was a Labour man, or so he made the claim,
And he told us at election time that decency was his aim.
He knew that Glasgow's housing was the very, very worst,
And he sought emancipation, one at a time – me first!!

WORKERS CITY

Mickie Kearns sought a licence and he didn't give a damn
If he had to pay a hundred pounds to grease a bailie's palm.
Says Inglis, "It's a hardship case. I'll put the news around,
Ah, but just tae prove your hardship, gimme seven hundred pounds."

On the 9th day of November in the year of '62
Mickie Kearns went to the Barrowland Bar some business for to do.
Johnny Inglis was a happy man when he came there an' all,
But the polis they were listening, and they went and burst the ball.

Ah, but people they are asking now, as people they will do,
If, Mickie Kearns, you will tell who showed the road to you.
For Inglis he has eighteen months to linger in a cell,
And we wonder if there's others maybe should be there as well.

J. N. REILLY

from Triptych

THERE IS A war on. Know your enemy.

In a room on the third floor of a tenement of dereliction, which was in darkness save for a cortege of whispering starlight and flickering horizon lights proceeding through the cracked and broken panes of the window like scents of bouquets, there was a boy. He pissed in the fireplace then picked up the small polythene bag which he had placed on the floor: littered with newspapers, crisp packets and cigarette ends. Holding the polythene bag over his nose and mouth, he repeatedly and rapidly inhaled and exhaled. This done, he smiled, tossed away the polythene bag, which was now empty of glue worth sniffing, and went over to the window.

The horizon was glittering like a Christmas tree, squirming with dancing girls in sequined leotards, lager advertisements, torn purple satin and explosions.

There is a war on. Know your enemy.

Corks popped from champagne bottles.

They are uncivilised. I mean, they simply do not know how to control their... eh...urges. You know, they are always having babies.

Troops kicked down the door and entered the house. Where are they? they demanded. They had received information, they said. She did not know. Where are who?

No more lies. We've had enough of lies.

Her husband was away working. She knew what was about to happen. Inwardly she asked her god why. Her son and two daughters were dragged screaming from their room. The troops wore the mercilessly cruel expressions of evil, anticipating events.

I mean, darling, one has to look after one's own.

I simply could not live without those afternoons at the Savoy.

Riots in London, Miami and Warsaw. Messages hanging from lampposts and escaping from glass skyscrapers. I looked at my hands. They have always looked old. I gazed around: slashed naked cubicles, confessions strapped to luxurious chairs, rainbowcoloured with fantasies of fucking appeared before us. I felt a stirring in my balls, saw butterflies fluttering from tenement windows and ragged children with moonlight in their pockets. A blue glow enveloped the boy and the room.

Pictures were disseminated as soon as available; acquired by the few intrepid journalists and adventurers who had dared cross the border.

The first survivor to be seen, knelt on the ground and wept.

You are correct. Arms. That is where the money is. I closed a deal for three thousand M.16s the other day. If you are seriously interested I shall introduce you to a few contacts.

Well, I have your daughter to keep. The profits from a corner shop would certainly not suffice to pay for the life she is accustomed to.

They laughed.

Quite right, my boy, quite right. And I must let you know, I have had an eye on you, and I think you will fare nicely in the business. I can detect a man who possesses what is required. And I am all for a little nepotism. Keep it in the family I say. Don't you think?

Indeed. Most definitely.

I have an appointment tomorrow. In Manchester, you understand. I think you should come along with me.

The bathwater drained, she stood in the bath, the steam rising from her. I dried her shoulders and back. While I was rubbing in the talcum powder, I discreetly unzipped my trousers and freed my prick. I then turned her around, put my arms around her hips and lifted her from the bath. I loosened my hold so that she slid slowly downwards and my prick was between her legs. We fucked against the wall.

More pictures of carnage and reports from survivors were laid on the table.

They shot my teenage son.

Sitting there in the dimness of the room with my back against the wall. I inhaled some more smoke and stood up. I went over to the window and gazed into the night. A myriad of great tubes intersecting at various angles and sprinkled with minute illuminated windows, appeared on the horizon and tapered into infinity. Angels fucking on tenement rooftops, the boy smiled at me.

If you get a sniff of that Soman, boy, you will wish you had never been born.

All police leave cancelled. Special courts set up to deal with rioters. There will be no limit to prison sentences. I closed the newspaper and began working.

I've had my share of fun, boy. I've seen things that would curl your spine. He laughed, scratched his crotch and pulled the boy towards himself.

The boy admired his gold wrist-watch and khaki safari jacket.

That's it, boy, nice and easy.

The boy sucked his prick, contemplating the machete on the rattan chair beside the bed.

You've never lived, boy. That's it you little fucker. Yes. I remember every minute of every campaign. A house in Sussex for me soon. That's it, get your tongue right up my arse, boy. You little fucker.

A British ship dumping radioactive waste in the Atlantic ocean. It was said that some the drums cracked open as they hit the sea. A Harwell scientist argued that you are more likely to be killed crossing the roads than by radioactivity. I bet my life on it, he concluded. As for the even more dangerous high-level radioactive waste, they do not know what to do with it. We will think of something, said a spokesman.

Police moved in on protestors.

He laid three twenty pound notes on the table. He breathed hard and waited for his wife's reaction. He did not know what to expect. He sat down on the hard-backed seat by the table so that she would not notice he was trembling. If he had stood any longer, he felt his legs would have folded beneath him.

Where did you get it? she asked, smiling, though ascertaining by her husband's demeanour that something was wrong.

Aren't you happy that I've brought home sixty quid?

Yes, but...

We need it, don't we. We've got a ninety pound electricity bill to pay. There's no way we can make up that sort of money from our social security money. And we've got to pay it. We need the electricity. We've got an eighteen month old baby sleeping through there, and by shit I'm not going to have the bastards cutting off our electricity. We can survive without it, but she can't. So I got us sixty quid. We've got forty saved, so now we can pay the fuckin' thing and have a ten spot extra.

Fine, fine, I told you something would turn up, but where did you get it?

He looked quickly around, as if to avoid her eyes, then rested his gaze on the glowing orange bars of the electric fire.

Well? Tell me. Did you steal it?

Yes.

Well what's the big deal? Did somebody see you? Where did you steal it from? Tell me what happened.

Okay, okay. When I was in the post office collecting the family allowance, I heard this old woman being cheeky to the girl serving her. I was in the queue next to the one she was in. Right? Well she was moaning at the girl for giving her a dirty twenty pound note. You don't expect me to take that, says she, I want a clean one. I couldn't believe it. Jesus, you would have thought she would have been grateful for the money, dirty or not. It wasn't even all that dirty. Anyway, I got the family allowance and she got a crisp twenty pound note to keep her other two company. I couldn't keep my eyes off her. Anyway, I found myself following her. I wasn't really thinking. I just kept saying to myself, I'll be having your purse, you ungrateful old bag. Well, I followed her past the semi-detached houses – you know the ones, that end where the new tenements begin, all on the same street – and I couldn't believe my luck. She walked along the path of the first tenement. I let her go into the close and I hurried on behind her. Not too quickly, so I wouldn't be noticed. She was on the stairs to the first landing. I pushed her onto her belly and told her to keep her mouth shut or I would batter her head in. My arm was practically covering her mouth by now, so she couldn't say much anyway. She was probably shit scared. I grabbed her handbag and opened it. She didn't just have sixty pounds but near on a hundred, maybe more, but all I was after were the sixty. I took it and beat it into the back court. I should have taken the lot. I knew everything I was doing. I went right because I knew I could sneak through other backcourts. If I had gone left I would have been out in the open with nowhere to run.

You madman. Did anybody see you?

No. I told you. No. It was easy.

She might have needed that money.

I didn't take all her money. She was an old bitch. I should have taken the lot. I could tell she wasn't short of a pound or two. I'm telling you, you should see some of the money those moaning-faced old bastards get in the post office. Some of them leave their pensions and whatever to accumulate then cash them, so they must have money to live on or they wouldn't be able to do that. You can always tell the poor old sods from the ones who are getting all sorts of pensions and allowances. And the poor ones have next to nothing, like us. You can always tell, and not just by looking at their clothes. But don't worry, I won't rob any more old folk, unless I'm certain they've plenty, and I mean rich.

You didn't hurt her, did you?

Just listen. There's no chance of me getting a job. Right? The money we can get from the social security is laughable. You know. We can hardly buy enough food, let alone pay electricity bills and buy clothes. When was the last time you bought a skirt for yourself, or a pair of shoes. We're always wearing the same gear. And when was the last time we went out for a night. Nearly a year.

I know, I know. Get to the point.

You know the point. I say I get involved with thieving. I've got it all worked out. The places, the times and the kind of people to rob. I'll only work on sure things, that I know I'll get away with. And with winter coming, the evenings will be darker which will help me. Then I'll be hidden by darkness. I've pissed around for too long.

When you feel the rush, when the heroin is racing through your veins, it's like ...eh...indescribable.

Tell us, sir, what does it feel like being a millionaire?

Just the same as being indigent, except one has more money.

At the first stroke, it will be...

Death for us all, that's what I'm saying, so long as you sit there doing nothing but watching t.v. and reading the daily shit. You must get out onto the street and let yourself be heard. Death for us all. Do you hear me? Are you listening? Do you care? Listen to this. Each Polaris submarine carries sixteen nuclear missiles. Each rocket has a range of 2,500 miles and carries H-bombs with an explosion capability of 600,000 tons of T.N.T. One Polaris submarine has the capacity to kill more people than all the bombs dropped during the second world war, which includes the A-bombs dropped on Hiroshima and Nagasaki. The Poseidon submarines carry up to sixteen missiles with ten warheads on each and they are more accurate than the Polaris submarines! And then there are the Trident submarines that carry twenty-four nuclear missiles. Do you realize that millions of people will be killed? That you will be one of them?

There is a war on. Know your enemy.

Friday night and all's well, the boy muttered to himself as he entered the living-room where his parents were sitting boozing.

Where have you been? his mother slurred at the sight of him.

Out and about, mother dearest, out and about.

You're a cheeky swine.

Do you think so, mother dearest.

Do you hear this cheeky swine? she called to his father.

He'll feel the back of my hand, grunted his father, turning his head slightly from the television before pouring a lager and a glass of whiskey for himself.

The boy went over to the settee where his father was stretched out and, shifting his father's legs, sat down.

You don't mind if I have a wee drink, he said, picking up and opening one of the numerous cans of extra strong lager which with a bottle of whisky, two packets of cigarettes and two ashtrays full to overflowing, occupied the coffee-table in front of the settee.

Who said you could take one of them?

I did, mother dearest, the prodigal son.

Do you hear this daft swine?

Aye, aye. Watch you lip, son. We had peace and quiet until you dragged your carcass in.

That's a can of lager you owe us, said his mother, and: Were you running around with that crowd of boys. You'll end up in the jail, you will.

Anything for eating, oh wonderful mother?

Aye, fresh air. Are you daft. It's Friday night, get yourself something from the chip shop.

Sorry, wonderful mother. I forgot it's fish supper day. Cross my palm with a note. A green one. Mind you, a red one will be accepted.

Do you hear this daft swine? Give him a quid.

His father threw a pound note at him.

Go and lose yourself, he said.

At the living-room door, the boy turned and said, Father dearest, oh great drunken sultana of the east, do you still screw that ugly bag? you're sick enough to.

He laughed. His father had not heard him, but his mother had.

Do you hear this daft swine? she shrieked, do you hear him?

The boy closed the living-room door and went into his sister's bedroom. She was sitting before her dressing-table, applying eye-shadow and wearing nothing but a pink floral bra and knickers.

Hi sis.

He laid himself on her bed.

You should knock before entering somebody's bedroom. I might have been naked.

All the better, beautiful sis. All the better.

What do you want? And I've no money to give you.

What's money, sis. I don't need money.

What do you want? I want to get dressed.

I don't want anything, sis.

Well, why did you come in here?

Just taking a stroll, sis, in the valley of death, and I fancied your beautiful company. Do you know we are all dying?

Why do you say horrible things like that. I think you like depressing everybody.

I don't, the opposite is true.

If you weren't my brother, I'd be scared of you. Do you know that?

He laughed.

I mean it.

She rose and went to her wardrobe, from which she picked a purple satinette dress, shirred at the breast.

Come on now, away you go and take your drugs and let me get dressed.

Drugs? beautiful sister. I want you to be my drug. How about some incest to heat you for the night?

I'm telling you, your head's pickled. Away you go.

Fine enough. Back to the streets I go, to the destruction, my pleasure and pain.

Where do you find those things to say? You should be on the stage.

Remember, beautiful sister, I'm with you and watching you everywhere you are.

He smiled and departed.

He was lying on his back. Between his legs, the boy was madly and speedily fucking him. He felt the semen rising. He was ready to ejaculate. The boy knew this and prepared to make his move. This is it. He began bellowing like a bull. As the semen began spurting onto his chest and face, the boy reached over to the rattan chair, picked up the machete and, with all his strength, thrust its blade under the man's ribs and pushed and pulled it from side to side before withdrawing and pulling on his trousers. He watched the blood dripping onto the bed and the semen trickling from the prick of this man whom he had been servant and sodomite to for the last month. He had hated him and could now truly rejoice in his cunning. He slapped his victim a few times, to be sure he was dead, before taking the watch from his wrist and picking up the khaki jacket and using it to wipe the semen from his face and chest. The jacket was too large for him, but that did not matter. He filled its pockets with the packets of cigarettes he helped himself to from the trunk. Ready to depart, he took what money he could find in the pockets of the dead man's trousers, grinned, and hurried off.

Yeah, it was fun.

I know what you mean. Why, we're doing them a favour. All their swollen bellies because of malnutrition. We used to puncture them with our bayonets. It passed the time. We were putting them out of their misery. They would have died anyway.

There were fears that deadly anthrax had escaped after a mysterious fire had ravaged a laboratory on the outskirts of the city. Firemen had to wear chemical suits to protect themselves.

Forty dangerous chemicals, there are all sorts of viruses in that building. We weren't going to take any chances.

A spokesman said that radioactive isotopes had not escaped, that they were, and are in metal containers in a concrete-lined fireproof room, that there was and is no cause for alarm.

They tied him to a lamppost and shot his knee-cap off in the name of freedom.

It was his fault. He's to blame.

I sawed the bastard's arm off.

Will you be my sweetheart?

You should have cut his balls off, more like.

You're taking too many chances, said his wife, counting the proceeds of his evening's operations. There were ninety-three pounds in all. Did everything run smoothly? I hope you're not being reckless.

Don't worry. I worked the bars. Friday night is pay night and that means drunk night. I robbed two guys tonight to get that money. Piss easy.

He laughed, lit a cigarette and:

I've got a plan to make us some big money. The only thing is that it will involve you. I could maybe do it by myself but I think it would be safer if you're my look -out. It will be a one-off job. We might make at least five hundred quid. What do you think?

I don't know.

Well there's this newsagent's. An old Pakistani runs it. At the best of times he's alone in the shop. Sometimes a young couple help him out but hardly ever.

It will be easy as long as we do everything as planned.

What about the baby?

We'll get your mother to look after her. We'll tell her we're going to the movies.

I suppose so.

You'll do it?

I suppose so. I'm really excited.

So am I.

And you really think we'll get away with it?

I'm positive.

You've got to make up your mind.

All right then. Yes. We do it. Do you fancy a cup of tea?

The boy had found a tattered easy chair in one of the adjoining rooms. Having dragged it over to the window, he sat down and, although the room was only dimly illuminated by the light from the street-lamps, rolled a joint of the marijuana he had acquired from an acquaintance. He would give him the money for it later. The effect of the marijuana exquisitely offset the effect of the cocaine he had been sniffing at his acquaintance's. Puffing on the joint he looked out of the window. Although it was winter, he did not feel the cold. He gazed into horizon, the past, present and future: dusty street messages in a distant sky rockets streaming tails of incandescence red with love affecting with bliss recurring amongst afternoon strolls exploding playing cards glittering signals drifting on the evening girl laughter naked breasts of forgotten names and days bleeding immortally.

The river is so polluted that the local people, their children and unborn children, are being infected by one or more of the following diseases: gastro-enteritis, dermatitis, hepatitis, diarrhoea, typhoid and polio. Who cares? you garbage pukers.

She played in the river that afternoon and woke the following morning covered in ulcers.

Missiles lit up the night sky.

It would cost too much to clean the river. We should need to expend five hundred million dollars over the next five years to make any impact on the pollution. Industries would have to be closed down. We couldn't do that. If we did, we should not have an economy.

Thanks for looking after her, mum. You don't know how grateful we are.

It's nothing. You need to go out and enjoy yourselves sometimes. Give me a shout any time. Cheeri-bye.

The door closed and locked behind her, they hurried into the living-room.

Where's the gear? he asked.

It's all here, look, replied his wife, lifting the shopping-bag containing their disguises from behind the couch and emptying it onto the rug in front of the fire, to set his mind at rest. The money, she said, impatient to see it and count it, for he had told her as they were walking away from the newsagent's that he was sure they had more than a thousand pounds, most of which he had taken from the shopkeeper's pockets.

Firstly he threw onto the rug the one, five and ten pound notes he had taken from the till, then four rolls of notes; each held together by rubber bands; which he had taken from the shopkeeper's pockets.

I told you, I told you. We've struck it rich.

She laughed and reached out to pick up one of the rolls.

No, count the loose notes first, then we'll count the rest.

From the till he had taken five ten pound notes, eight five pound notes and sixteen one pound notes. Of the rolls, one was of eight hundred and forty-four one pound notes and the others respectively five hundred and twenty-two five pound notes, one hundred and thirteen ten pound notes and thirty-six twenty pound notes. In all, a tally of five thousand four hundred and ten pounds.

I can't believe it. She knelt gazing at the piles of money between them.

Neither can I. But here it is. Maybe it being Saturday, this is the week's takings, that he forgot to take to the bank. That must be it.

I thought maybe a thousand or so if we were lucky, but this...

Yes. We'll have to be careful with it. We can't go spending it here, there and everywhere, or people will begin to wonder why we've got so much money, especially with me being unemployed. But so we can get some benefit from it, what we'll do is this. We need a washing machine, right, so we go and buy one but on a hire purchase agreement. It will cost more money that way, but at least we know we've got the money to meet with monthly payments. That way we won't attract suspicion. We also need clothes, so what we'll do is buy something every now and then. We'll get a good living from it if we take it easy. Remember, we'll still be getting our social security benefits.

We'll certainly be able to sleep a lot easier now. It's good to know for certain we can pay our heating bills and rent and won't have to do without food. It's a miracle.

You're right, and I won't need to go out robbing folk for six months, maybe a year.

We're in the money, we're in the money.

I didn't say that.

I did.

Sometimes I lie back and let the boat drift, through the clear blue rushes and the movement of smaller animals on the banks, or else I dip into the water and swim for a while in geometric pleasure.

I rowed through the shades of evening, the stillness, the implication of forgotten tongues twining around floral scents came night. I pulled by boat ashore, onto the bank of eternity, illumined by starlight and thoroughly refreshed, I lay down.

A rocket in the distance.

There is a war on. Know your enemy.

They are all around, in buses, in cars and tenements, counting out their avaricious dreams, so apathetic they stop and stare at the blood, counting out their avaricious dreams, they will betray you for a television or a nine to five lobotomy, or murder you and your family in the name of a god or liberty. I tell you, I want to apply myself to the pleats in her skirt and the creases in my sheets, but no, not just now, no rest for you, you bastards. Sit up, shit eaters, and you look in this direction and see the slavish Charlie turning folk away from checkpoints, folk running from the bloody pernicious fist of totalitarianism. Charlie dressed in red and blue guarding a long row of companies spreading diseases, starving bellies and minds, arming for oblivion, that's your Sickles and Stripes, bomb-toting Charlie carving them up, eh Charlie, hear them scream like stuck pigs. I tell you, if I believed in a god I would thank that god for sunrises and sunsets, ghostly moons all swirling mists and forests at night, oh yes, and a little boy dropping his ice cream on the road, girls smiling in bikinis and the stars glittering over the squalor of tenements, damp and steaming streets, my darling, if I believed in a god I would thank that god for my faith in spite of evil churchmen and statesmen, venal senators and ministers, so indignant and pious, licking manicured claws and ensanguined jaws, rapaciously praying, in the names of Christ and Marx and Moses, on their crusades of crucifixion once again I earnestly admonish, if I believed in a god I would thank that god for bestowing in me the will to retain my sanity amidst the miserable, drunk and ignorant, the Saturday night heroes, those quotidian people dissembling before televisions and mirrors and auntie Main the machiolated: Bring back the birch, hang the bastards: and the laughter from the shadows, girls and boys stoned by parents, teachers, radios, magazines, pills, dreams hold on, wait a moment, listen, howling dogs in the night, the sound of shattering glass in the distance, pipes and engines. and the warmth of her softly breathing the yawning scents of dawn, an ornithic aubade adorned with the eternal here in my room the white net curtains gently swaying.

JAMES D. YOUNG

Culture and Socialism: Working-Class Glasgow, 1778-1978

> Sexless, ageless, classless, nationless he/she is the all-important nothing of middle-class wisdom.
>
> *Royden Harrison*

WE ARE GATHERED at the People's Palace, Glasgow, on Thursday, 3 September, to inaugurate Ken Currie's magnificent pictorial ode to all rebels, martyrs, fugitives and anti-capitalist saints and sinners in Glasgow between 1778 and 1978. The inauguration of this mural history of Glasgow ranging over a period of two hundred years is a unique occasion for creative, poetic, artistic, intellectual, and *radical Scotland:* an occasion for celebration and resurrection. Because the Left in Scotland has usually had to function in a hostile and philistine environment for a prolonged historical period, the radicals and socialists have always responded to massive poverty, inequality and class-engendered injustice by girning and flyting. But this is not an occasion for girning or flyting. It is rather an occasion for celebrating what the Scottish working-class movement has achieved, what it is achieving and what it will achieve in the years to come, Thatcher or no Thatcher.

Although the result of the general election in June, 1987, means that the Scots are now standing at a crossroads-crisis marked 'national extinction' at the hands of the multinational corporations or 'national re-birth' under the inspiration of our centuries-old radical tradition and outward-looking internationalism, Ken Currie's mural history of working-class Glasgow is another major sign of our growing confidence and self-confidence. It is also a permanent landmark in the ongoing cultural revolution in late-twentieth-century Scotland.

What Ken Currie has achieved as an artist cannot be separated from political development in contemporary Scotland, though the relationships between the two are neither simple nor immediately obvious. This is important because in a recent article in the *Sunday Telegraph* entitled 'Can the Tories govern Scotland?', Norman Stone, the Glaswegian Thatcherite, attributed the Scottish Tories electoral annihilation to 'the decline of Imperial consciousness'.[1] Yet he deliberately ignored the cultural, spiritual and intellectual resurgence in this small corner of the modern world.

But if the connections between the resurgence in contemporary culture and politics are not obvious, there are identifiable links between what is happening in Scotland today and Scottish history. From the Reformation onwards, there were powerful negative and positive factors operating within Scottish society. The country was very poor by comparison with England; and the Scottish ruling class did not really encourage artistic or cultural endeavour. This specific, concrete material environment and heritage had a profound influence on the development of the history of radicalism in Scotland between 1778 and 1978.

As Frederick Engels always insisted: 'There is no great historical evil without a compensating historical progress'. And the Scots' centuries-old *material* poverty gave them an intense interest in theology and philosophy, a passion for the 3 Rs, and an argumentative, disputatious disposition. In the eighteenth century, this intellectual and cultural heritage allowed them to become the pioneers of modern economics, sociology, a rudimentary psychology and Utopian socialism. The 'contradictions' of modern capitalism were very sharp in the City of Glasgow. By the late nineteenth century, Scottish socialists were more successful than their English or French counterparts in disseminating and popularising Marxian economics among working-class men and women.

In surveying the history of socialist movements throughout the world before the First World War, Edward Roux, the South African socialist, said that Glasgow and Chicago had produced more socialist literature than any other cities in the world.[2] In an article published in an American socialist magazine in 1941, it was asserted that Glasgow had been 'the intellectual centre of British labour' in the 1930s.[3] The Scottish workers' movement was, in fact, reflecting the *national* environment in which it had been shaped from 1778 onwards.

In the 1930s the Scottish working-class movement produced important socialist novelists and poets – James Barke, James Welsh, Lewis Grassic Gibbon and Hugh MacDiarmid. The socialists in Scotland were now encouraging and fostering socialist poetry and doggerel. And out of the working-class struggle for better wages and better social conditions a market – a huge market – was created for the chapbooks and doggerel of John S. Clarke and Tom Anderson. There were also attempts to develop a workers' theatre and a left-wing cinema.

Yet despite the first significant artistic and cultural stirrings in Glasgow in the 1920s and 1930s, the labour movement did not have the material resources to encourage, assist or commission a Scottish Diego Rivera. Indeed in 1938, when Hugh MacDiarmid first published 'The Red Scotland Thesis', he complained quite bitterly about 'the philistine 'common sense'', and the 'self-satisfied anti-intellectualism' in the Scottish working-class movement. In Hugh MacDiarmid's opinion, Guy Aldred – and this in spite of Aldred's anti-Stalinism and agitation for a Fourth International – was the only socialist writer in Glasgow who was worth reading. As MacDiarmid summed up: 'His (Aldred's)

'Bakunin House' has long been a tower of liberty and justice in the otherwise unredeemed cultural chaos of Glasgow.'[4]

When he published *Scottish Studies* in 1926, Hugh MacDiarmid had argued that 'in music as in drama we (the Scots) are unique in the fact that we have practically failed to develop any worth considering at all'. He attributed the absence of a national tradition of any great music or drama to Calvinism and 'the comparative material poverty of our country'.[5] He did not say anything at all about painting or the pictorial arts.

Mexico was a much more poverty-stricken country than Scotland in the 1930s, and yet the Mexicans produced the great painter and revolutionary socialist, Diego Rivera. In producing magnificent murals of scenes from Mexican history – of the bitter and bloody struggles of the peasants and workers – Rivera became one of the great painters of the twentieth century. But there were two concrete reasons for the emergence of Diego Rivera. In the first place, there was a long tradition of painting murals in Mexico long before this all-round, multi-talented, almost renaissance man, came on the scene. Secondly, he could not have achieved what he did without the moral, spiritual and financial support of the workers' movement in Mexico and America. Furthermore, the crucial importance of socialist institutions and a supportive culture did not detract from – or belittle – Rivera's genius.

To the best of my knowledge Hugh MacDiarmid and Diego Rivera never met or corresponded with each other. Yet they both understood the revolutionary role of art, culture and poetry in the struggle for democracy, justice and socialism. In explaining the connection between the workers' struggle for better material conditions and culture, Walter Benjamin, the German socialist and victim of fascism, wrote: 'The class struggle, which is always present to a historian influenced by Marx, is a fight for the crude material things without which no refined and spiritual things could exist'.[6] And yet Benjamin fought as few socialists have fought for an appreciation of the finer spiritual things in life.

A major reason for the absence of a Scottish Diego Rivera was the terrible mass unemployment, poverty, malnutrition, deprivation and ill-health. As socialists have always argued, the imaginative faculty depends on a reasonable material and spiritual environment. In 1938 Hugh MacDiarmid also wrote about 'the disproportionately terrible social and economic conditions of Scotland compared with England and of the absolute needlessness of anything of the sort'.[7] Capitalism was always more harsh, rapacious and brutal in Scotland than in England. Because they existed within a much poorer country, the Scots were more preoccupied with a struggle for the crude material things.

By the 1930s the first serious stirrings of working-class and socialist activity in drama and music were evident in Glasgow. The philistine bourgeoisie in Glasgow were much more interested in making profits and arms and in encouraging the dictators in Italy, Spain and Germany than in assisting artists, poets or prophets. Those who tried to make a living by writing novels or biographies had a very tough time; and the poverty-haunted Grassic Gibbon depended on Americans to buy the novels in which he portrayed working-class Scotland. But Gibbon did at least stimulate the middle-class dunces in Aberdeen to coin one immortal phrase: 'Him write a book. I kent his faither'.

The cultural chaos that Hugh MacDiarmid saw in Glasgow in the 1930s has now gone; and it has been replaced by a socialist- inspired cultural revival, a resurgence and a vitality in historiography, poetry, literature, drama, the cinema, painting and the arts. Modern capitalism is coming to an end in the Western world; and the working classes from Nicaragua to Scotland are displaying a new self-confidence despite the brutality of the Thatchers and the Reagans. As Grassic Gibbon said in one of the last essays he wrote before his death in 1934: 'Towards the culmination of a civilisation the arts, so far from decaying, always reach their greatest efflorescence'.[8]

Pat Lally, the leader of the Glasgow District Council, has described Ken Currie's mural history as a major work of popular art. Moreover, this major work of popular art does not just represent a comparatively new and major talent in Scottish painting, although it does that vividly, graphically and visually in a permanent form. It is also a much deeper *national* expression of the forces of change and the voices of revolt against philistine money-grubbing at the expense of human dignity, creativity, curiosity, individual vitality and autonomy.

The good book tells us that 'where there is no vision, the people perish'. Yet despite the Scots' historic deficiences in music, drama and the pictorial arts, the Scots portrayed in Ken Currie's mural history of Glasgow did not lack vision. The vision was there in the speeches, writings and agitations of Thomas Muir of Huntershill, in the struggles of the Black weaver, Mathew Bogie, who was one of the leaders of the Radical War of 1820, and in the superb pedagogy of 'the great John MacLean'. And in our own times, the vision of a better society was seen in the UCS sit-in.

When I had the privilege of living in the home of Eugene V. Debs, the great American socialist described by Guy Aldred as 'America's vision-maker', in Terre Haute, Indiana, in 1980, I encountered and enjoyed the murals dedicated to Debs' fruitful life of struggle for justice and socialism. But Ken Currie has not just portrayed the lives of great individuals. He has, in fact, portrayed the lives and struggles of the working class in Glasgow – a magnificent *class* in a magnificent *City* – over a period of two hundred years.

To appreciate the unique scale and scope of Ken Currie's artistic achievement and vision from a socialist perspective, we must yet again glance at what Walter Benjamin, the German authority on art and culture, had to say about the most important aspect of developing socialist *images* of the world around us:

Not man or men but the struggling, oppressed class itself is the depository of historical knowledge. In Marx it appears as the last enslaved class, as the avenger that completes the liberation in the name of generations of the downtrodden.

Furthermore, in describing what separated socialists from Social Democrats, Benjamin criticised the right-wing elements in the labour movement for portraying the working class as 'the redeemer of the future generations'. In summing up, he said: 'This training made the (German) working class forget both its hatred and its spirit of sacrifice, for both are nourished by the image of the *enslaved ancestors* rather than that of liberated grandchildren'.[9] The dominant *socialist image* in this mural history of Glasgow is the unbroken image of our 'enslaved ancestors' within a specific national setting.

In 1957 John McLeish, a brilliant psychologist from Glasgow, contributed an article to the magazine, *Universities and Left Review*. The article culminated with an unanswered but not rhetorical question: 'Scotland a nation once again or the workers' international?' But in 1987 the forces of socialist internationalism outside of Scotland are telling us that the survival of the Scottish nation is the pre-condition for a socialist-humanist society in this small part of the world. And the most intelligent, imaginative, creative and radical Scots have always given a sympathetic ear to the democratic forces in the outside world from the French Revolution in 1789, right through to the Russian Revolution of 1917 and the Revolution in Nicaragua today.

What Ken Currie's mural history of Glasgow conveys to us is that the Scots have been exiled inside their own country. For when a people have no access to their own real history, they are exiles. However, this mural history of Glasgow between 1778 and 1978 is proof of the profound changes occurring in Scottish artistic, cultural and political life. By forcing their way into the national culture, the murals of Ken Currie depicting the historic struggles of working-class men and women, together with other facets of contemporary working-class cultural activity, are feeding back into Scottish life and impinging on the political consciousness of socialists and trade unionists.

This was brought home to me when I visited my friend Harry McShane, the veteran Clydeside socialist, at Baxter House, exactly a week ago. Within minutes of my arrival, he showed me a letter that he was sending to Mrs. Thatcher. In this historic letter, he told Thatcher-Victoria that a Scottish Assembly was the very minimum change being demanded by the working-class movement. In informing me that he now favoured national independence rather than mere Devolution, Harry was expressing something much deeper than himself. This is simply another expression of 'the new passions and the new forces' represented in the new mural history of working-class Glasgow.

In the recent article in the *Sunday Telegraph,* Norman Stone observed with some sadness and nostalgia for the days of the Empire that the Tories in Scotland

re now a 'foreign', 'patrician' group of outsiders. He might have added that
hey are full of bare-faced cheek. But this is not a new development at all. The
eal culture of the Scottish nation – not just the fight for crude material things,
ut the deep unconquerable spirituality of the producers of wealth – is depicted
y Ken Currie. As Scotland increasingly moves towards self-determination, the
ew attempts to rehabilitate such reactionary obscurantists as Henry Dundas,
he Dictator of the 1790s, will fail because the Tories in Scotland are now naked,
xposed and indecent.

Contemporary Scotland is not just beginning to come of age as it moves
owards self-government. It is simultaneously reaching out to 'the Age of
Reason' anticipated by Tom Paine and Thomas Muir of Huntershill. What is
appening in Scotland is a part of the international revolt that we have seen in
Nicaragua and South Africa. But even in the heartlands of capitalism, the 'new
assions and new forces' are agitating for a People's art, a People's history and a
People's culture.

In recent years I have been privileged to attend conferences on working-class
istory in Austria, West Germany and America. Despite the formidable
obstacles facing socialists in those countries, they have done much to promote
eft-wing films, poetry, literature, drama and murals portraying the history of
he really important people in their own societies – the producers of wealth, not
he parasites.

But in Austria the Labour Party has created its own choirs and choral
ocieties. Despite the enormous number of influential fascist sympathisers in the
uling circles in Vienna, local Labour administrations have had streets and
quares named after such famous socialists as Otto Bauer. In the Austrian
niversities the socialists' intellectual, artistic and cultural achievements and
nti-fascist struggles are acknowledged and recognised as a part of the national
ulture. As I was preparing this talk, it occurred to me that the most accurate
uide to the *degree* of democracy in any contemporary society is the *continuous
presence* – or the continuous absence – of working-class struggles in drama,
ilms, street-names and murals.

Although the socialists in West Germany have agitated and worked in a less
ympathetic and favourable environment than their Austrian counterparts, they
ave begun to make some impression on the dominant culture. In 1968 the
overnment of the West German Federal Republic asserted that the
ssassination of Rosa Luxemburg in 1919 had been in accordance with martial
aw, though no charges had been made against her and no trial had taken place.
Rosa was – even in death – 'the enemy within'. Yet West Germany with its
errible fascist legacy is changing; and militant, democratic socialists are saying
hat socialists have to say in the universities and research institutes.

In 1985 an international cultural festival celebrating the contribution of
Antonio Gramsci and Rosa Luxemburg to human knowledge, culture and

advancement was held in Hamburg. It attracted artists, painters, historians and film-makers from all over the world; and it was funded by official sources and, in turn, generated profit and stimulated other cultural projects. Next year a group of socialist scholars are hosting an international congress on the work of Upton Sinclair, the American novelist and author of *The Jungle,* in order to discuss and assess the relationship between socialism, literature and the arts.

In America socialists and radicals have published major biographies of Daniel De Leon and Eugene V. Debs. Just as the Scots and the West Germans have forced the authorities to confront the issue of the systematic persecution of John Maclean and Roso Luxemburg, so the Americans are succeeding in securing the gradual rehabilitation of Gene Debs. By 1979 John Joseph Laska had completed his murals celebrating the achievements of the man who on five different occasions stood for election as the Socialist Party's Presidential candidate. The murals paying tribute to Debs' life and martyrdom in the cause of American and international Labour are in the attic of the Debs' home in Terre Haute. Moreover, the Debs' home is now classified as 'a National Parks Department Historic Site'. As Glasgow prepares to become the cultural capital of Europe in 1990, perhaps we could do something to secure Labour's 'martyred dead' even greater recognition in the schools and culture of Scotland's most energetic City.

One of the questions I have asked myself during the last few days is this: 'What united the multitude of individuals portrayed in the murals painted by Ken Currie?' It would be comforting to suggest that they were all socialists. However, it simply would not be true. In the technical language of academic historians, the working class in Scotland before 1832 belonged to 'the pre-industrial' working class. But what the Scottish men and women portrayed in the eight panels of murals had in common was a passion for justice and freedom – a preoccupation more often than not with the crude material things as a pre-condition for art, culture and dignity. What they also had in common was a hatred of Absolutism, arbitrary authority, tyranny, injustice and hierarchy.

To understand the importance of the contribution to human advancement made by the individuals portrayed in Ken Currie's murals between 1778 and 1850, we should remember that it was an era of rising 'bourgeois individualism' when ordinary people were regarded by ruling classes everywhere as un-persons whose poverty was a part of the natural order of things. In the eighteenth century, for example, the 'great' Samuel Johnson told James Boswell: 'You are to consider that it is our duty to maintain the subordination of civil society; and where there is a gross or shameful deviation from rank, it should be punished so as to deter others from making the same perversion'.[11] In the late 1840s Thomas Carlyle attacked working people for asking questions about the 'natural' hierarchy in the world. As he expressed it: 'Recognised or not, a man has his superiors, a regular hierarchy above him, extending upwards, degree by degree, to Heaven itself and God the maker, who made this world not for anarchy but for rule and order'.[12]

From the 1880s, when modern socialism was born, to the UCS sit-in in 1971, the presence of the socialist vision of the better world to come has been a constant factor in Scottish – and English, German, French, Italian and American – working-class struggles. In what is perhaps the best available definition of socialism in any language, Theodor Shanin says: 'Socialism is about ending the domination of people by other people, about collectivism which is nobody's prison, about social justice and equality, about making people conscious of their power and ability to control their destinies here and now'. This is the vision which united all of the colourful individuals portrayed by Ken Currie over a period of two hundred years; and this is what we are celebrating tonight as we look in the direction of what Antonio Gramsci, the Italian socialist, described as 'the City of the future'.

We should acknowledge the determination and the hard, sustained work undertaken by Elspeth King and Michael Donnelly in helping in the birth of this work of popular art; and we should not be afraid to trumpet our socialist opinions from the rooftops, the squares and the market-places of this hard-working, honest and very cheeky City. And is doing so, it is appropriate to recall the words of the young American novelist, Norman Mailer:

> We want a socialist world not because we have the conceit that men would therefore be happy...but because we feel the moral imperative in life itself to raise the human condition, even if this should ultimately mean no more than that man's suffering has been lifted to a higher level.

FOOTNOTES

1. Norman Stone, 'Can the Tories govern Scotland?', *Sunday Telegraph,* 14 June 1987.

2. Eddie and Win Roux, *Rebel Pity* (London, 1970), p.7.

3. Britannicus, 'The 'New International' in England', *The New International,* July 1941.

4. Hugh MacDiarmid, 'The Red Scotland Thesis', *The Voice of Scotland,* Vol.1, No.1, 1938.

5. Hugh MacDiarmid, *Scottish Studies* (Edinburgh, 1926).

6. Walter Benjamin, *Illuminations* (London, 1977).

7. MacDiarmid, 'The Red Scotland Thesis', op. cit.

8. Hugh MacDiarmid, 'Lewis Grassic Gibbon', *Little Reviews Anthology 1946* (London, 1946).

9. Benjamin, op. cit.

10. John McLeish, 'The Uses of Literacy', *Universities and Left Review,* Summer 1957.

11. *James Boswell's Life of Johnson,* edited J. Brady (New York, 1968).

12. Thomas Carlyle, *Chartism* (London, 1960).

HAMISH HENDERSON

IN 1973, IN their jointly written foreward to *Homage to John MacLean,* T. S. Law and Thurso Berwick concluded: "In the matter of whom do we remember and how do we remember him, the poets always have the last word, something which politicians among others should always remember." It is a pleasing thought and undoubtedly true. How we apprehend the past – its people and their times – is largely in the hands of the poets. It is as true for Wallace and Bruce in the song of Harry the Minstrel and the epic of John Barbour as for Ilium on the breath of Homer. It is as true for Sidmouth and Castlereagh in Shelley's *Mask of Anarchy* as for those 'transformed utterly' in Yeats' great *Easter 1916.* This is the heart and soul of all history.

Harold MacMillan, Prime Minister in the early 1960s, and his War Minister, John Profumo, and the Premier's dear friend from across the Atlantic, the millionaire president Jack Kennedy who thought the nuclear "coont doon" he embarked on was "the best poker game in the world", and the CIA-sponsored Moral Rearmers or Buchmanites (who turned Jesus on his heid and made the upper classes, the "up-and-outs" as Buchman caad them, the new, mair refined, salt o the earth) – all these should be remembered as Hamish Henderson so stylishly and with such withering acumen depicts them here in this masterpiece of social-political invective. In *Jimmy Tyrie* the politicians, the plutocrat bankers, the religious conmen, the "bullyboy" yanks, the reptile fuzz and their narks, and the Polaris depot-ship Hunley, that "daith wish (nae mine!)" – all have to come crawling out of the slime in their true colours and be named truly for what they really are. The poet leaves them no room to hide in, the glitter and the masquerade are at an end for all of them. This song was sung by those who sat down "close together" at the Holy Loch anti-nuclear protests of the early 1960s and for many years thereafter. It is a mocking extravaganza of great power and it encapsulates a whole world of political and military evil, as well as the brave defiance of marchers and pickets, in just one or two deceptively simple but masterly strokes. Its language is of the people but with no vestige of the snuffling propriety of the place-seeking Leftie. Its politics is implacably of the streets. It is a call for the massed solidarity of working-class people, man and woman, old and young, against the death machine in our midst. It is history living up to poetry.

Jimmy Tyrie

I saw Macmillan doon the toon.
Wha's that, my dearie?
That's aul' Blundermac
Hey, Jimmy Tyrie
Blundermac, Scabbytash
That's a', my dearie.
If you sit close tae me, I winna weary.

I saw a Tory doon the toon
Wha's that, my dearie?
That's a boneheid
Hey, Jimmy Tyrie
Boneheid, Blundermac, Scabbytash
That's a', my dearie.
If you sit close tae me, I winna weary.

I saw Profumo doon the toon.
Wha's that, my dearie?
That's a Poodlefaker
Hey, Jimmy Tyrie
Poodlefaker, Boneheid, Blundermac,
    Scabbytash
That's a', my dearie.
If you sit close tae me, I winna weary.

I saw a Yankee by the Loch.
Wha's that, my dearie?
That's a Bullyboy
Hey, Jimmy Tyrie
Bullyboy, Poodlefaker, Boneheid,
    Blundermac, Scabbytash
That's a', my dearie.
If you sit close tae me, I winna weary.

I saw a polis by the Loch.
Wha's that, my dearie?
That's a Croakerjack
Hey, Jimmy Tyrie

Croakerjack, Bullyboy, Poodlefaker,
　　Boneheid, Blundermac, Scabbytash
That's a', my dearie.
If you sit close tae me, I winna weary.

I saw a nark abuin the brae.
Wha's that, my dearie?
That's a Hornygolloch
Hey, Jimmy Tyrie
Hornygolloch, Croakerjack, Bullyboy,
　　Poodlefaker, Boneheid, Blundermac,
　　Scabbytash
That's a', my dearie.
If you sit close tae me, I winna weary.

I saw a blubbin' Buchmanite.
Wha's that, my dearie?
That's a Bamstick
Hey, Jimmy Tyrie
Bamstick, Hornygolloch, Croakerjack,
　　Bullyboy, Poodlefaker, Boneheid,
　　Blundermac, Scabbytash
That's a', my dearie.
If you sit close tae me, I winna weary.

I saw a banker on his knees.
Wha's that, my dearie?
That's a Buttonpusher
Hey, Jimmy Tyrie
Buttonpusher, Bamstick, Hornygolloch,
　　Croakerjack, Bullyboy, Poodlefaker,
　　Boneheid, Blundermac, Scabbytash
That's a', my dearie.
If you sit close tae me, I winna weary.

I saw Jack a-tellin' his beads.
Wha's that, my dearie?
That's a Coonter-doon
Hey, Jimmy Tyrie
Coonter-doon, Buttonpusher, Bamstick,
　　Hornygolloch, Croakerjack, Bullyboy,
　　Poodlefaker, Boneheid, Blundermac,

Scabbytash
That's a', my dearie.
If you sit close tae me, I winna weary.

I saw the Hunley on the Loch.
Whit's that, my dearie?
That's a Daith Wish
Hey, Jimmy Tyrie
Daith Wish (nae mine!), Coonter-doon,
   Buttonpusher, Bamstick, Hornygolloch,
   Croakerjack, Bullyboy, Poodlefaker,
   Boneheid, Blundermac, Scabbytash
That's a', my dearie.
If you sit close tae me, I winna weary.

Croakerjack: *bullfrog*
Horneygolloch: *centipede*

Further Notes on Authors

FREDDY ANDERSON

...is in a distinguished line of East End poets going back to Alexander (Sandy) Rodger, the apprentice weaver in Bridgeton, and Willie Miller, the cabinetmaker from Parkhead, who wrote the world famous nursery song *Wee Willie Winkie* round about 1860. Freddy, originally from Monaghan, has a great love for what the Scots call *smeddum* (spirit and gumption) and those who possess it, an inveterate detestation for the Welch (sic) rabbit Kinnock, his choc-box wife Glenys and their slobbering soul-mate Hattersley, and a long-held belief that all governments should be clerks at the service of the people. His play *Krassivy* won the Best Fringe Play Award at Edinburgh in 1980. Two other plays, *Oiny Hoy* (adapted from his unpublished novel) and *The Calton Weavers* were big hits at Glasgow Mayfest in 1987 and transferred successfully to the Edinburgh International Festival the same year. A volume of verse, *At Glasgow Cross and Other Poems* (Fat Cat Publications, 1987) is in its second print run.

PETER ARNOTT

...hails from Edinburgh but has mostly lived and worked in Glasgow in recent years. He is a dramatist with a goodly number of stage successes to his name, the best known probably being the *Benny Lynch* play. He has done a lot of good work in community drama with his friend Peter Mullan and Rutherglen Drama Group.

DOMINIC BEHAN

...came to Glasgow when he was fifteen years old. He was a friend of Hamish Henderson's and Hugh MacDiarmid – each of whom he can think of as mentor. MacDiarmid pays compliment to Behan in his book *The Company I've Kept*. Behan has worked for the BBC Third programme, but never managed – as was his mother's dearest wish – to get on the first. He and Jim McLean are old and close friends and live, we are led to believe, in each other's pockets: Behan being the older, ergo, closer. They share most things including the same politics and literary outlook. Behan's real life's work is spreading dissent, be it bibulous or bibliographical. He and Freddy Anderson and Matt McGinn spent a youth together, and Behan thinks that it didn't do him a great deal of harm – what it did for Freddy and Matt, Dominic is not disposed to say. He is the author of many songs and strikes and plays. He is at present writing a biography of his friend,

Spike Milligan, in the daytime, and at night praying for Mrs Thatcher with such a vengeance that the knees are worn out of his arse.

JOHN TAYLOR CALDWELL

...was born in Whiteinch, Glasgow, in 1911, the son of a tailor and a Co-op shop assistant. In 1915 the family moved to Belfast, where John received his schooling, leaving at 13 and returning to Glasgow. For a couple of years he worked as a pageboy in a cinema; then for eleven years as a bellboy and steward on the Anchor Line. Caldwell had a natural interest in political philosophy, and in current politics. In 1938 he made his last voyage and went working full-time with the *United Socialist Movement* (founded by Guy Aldred). In 1939 he joined with Aldred, Jane Patrick and Ethel MacDonald in opening the Strickland Press in George Street, Glasgow. He worked on the press, on a family, non-wage basis, for the next thirty years, taking over editorship of *The Word* on Guy's death in 1962. Caldwell opposed the Second World War. Refusing to accept conditional exemption, he appeared before the Tribunal twice and was eventually granted total exemption. During his retirement from active work in the Movement, Caldwell has collected and collated the *Writings of Guy A. Aldred* and prepared them for publication on microfilm. He has also written a biography of Aldred: *Come Dungeons Dark* – which includes chapters on the persecution and vicious imprisonment of conscientious objectors during the First World War. The book is published by Luath Press, Barr, Ayrshire.

ALEX CATHCART

...was born in Kinning Park in 1943. He has worked in various occupations in various parts of the world. He now lives and writes in Linwood, a defunct dormitory town built for the workers of the now flattened Rootes car plant to eat, sleep and reproduce in. After publication of his first novel, *The Comeback* (Polygon, 1986), Alex received a Scottish Arts Council Bursary which enabled him to complete his second novel, *The Missionary*, published by Polygon this year. A third is in progress. The novels deal with many of the themes raised in this anthology.

HAMISH HENDERSON

...was born in Blairgowrie, Perthshire, in 1919. During World War II he served with the 51st (Highland) Division at Alamein and in Italy. He is a Founder Member (1951) of the School of Scottish Studies at Edinburgh University.

SANDY HOBBS

...was born in Aberdeen in 1937. He was worked in Dundee, Glasgow and Edinburgh. He is at present teaching Psychology at Paisley College. Over the years Sandy has been a member of various left-wing organisations, but currently is attached to none. He has published widely, mainly on psychology, education and popular culture, in journals such as New Society, Oral History, Psychological Record, and the Scottish Educational Review.

R. D. LAING

...was born in the Govanhill area in 1927. In pre-war Glasgow everything south of Eglinton Toll was middle-class suburbia where the Victorian ethos – instilled with the belt, the hymn, the piano lesson and the fee-paying school – took no prisoners. Govanhill was, in point of fact, little better than a kind of genteel slum, but its not-heard children, its sombre, well-kept closes and above all its belief in its own sorely tested respectability, set it apart. An Irishman of my acquaintance swears there used to be policemen at the Toll turning back any saunterers from the Gorbals who wished to continue on a bit further. The factual truth of this may be questionable, but he has caught unerringly a more elusive truth – the *feel* of that time and that place. That Laing ever managed to transcend these class barriers is an achievement in itself. And who can say why Laing and not the myriad others of his class and profession in whose every self-protective manoeuvre you can read their life-long fear and hatred of the lumpen 'scruff'? Is it just personal temperament or luck in the people we meet or perhaps a bit of both? Early on Laing was friendly with the much more experienced Karl Abenheimer (a non-mental psychotherapist here in Glasgow) whose critical approach to the whole concept of mental illness might well have been Laing's springboard. But let's rejoice it did indeed happen, however it happened. Laing's genius is for stripping away the callous anti-life assumptions and absurdities of conventional psychiatric practice which is based on purely medical models. It is a fight against the threat of a deadening conformity, and it is our fight too.

ROBERT LYNN

...was born in the Calton, Glasgow, in 1924, and went to St Mungo's Academy. After his apprenticeship in Yarrow's, he joined the merchant service and sailed as an Engineer Officer. An Anarchist from the age of twenty, and a firm believer in the supreme efficacy of Direct Action in the fight against oppression, Robert can point to many successful outcomes in the struggle he has waged all his life – at sea, in industry, in prisons. He looks forward to the social revolution, but meantime he lives it in his own day-to-day engagement with life, and his refusal to make peace with the System.

JOHN McGARRIGLE

...is yet another exile from the Gorbals. He now lives and writes in Castlemilk and helped form the Castlemilk Writers' Workshop.

JANETTE McGINN

...lives in Rutherglen and was employed as organiser of the Castlemilk Citizens' Advice Bureau between 1978 and 1984. During the 'Gizza Hoose' campaign of 1983 she supported the tenants in their protest.

IAN McKECHNIE

...was born in Anderston, Glasgow, in 1938. He served as a Regular soldier in Cyprus between 1956 and 1958 at the height of the war against EOKA. This robbed him of any illusions he may have had regarding the beneficence of Empire. On quitting the army Ian developed an interest in grassroots political activity, and alongside this a passion for literature and music. There has never been any question of conflict between these interests. Each constantly sustains the other, he believes; each giving the other extra scope and an added dimension. Ian believes there is sanity in diversity. I'll drink to that. Must acknowledge a debt to him here for the moral support, the practical advice and the help in a hundred different ways which was there for the asking during the preparation of this book.

BRENDAN McLAUGHLIN

...worked as a telephone engineer before going to Strathclyde University in 1978. He graduated with Honours in Arts and Social Science in 1982. He writes stories and songs and, until more recent times, was a frequent performer singing with guitar in pubs and clubs in and around Glasgow.

JIM McLEAN

...spent a term in Barlinnie at the time of National Service rather than serve in the British army. He is a Scottish Socialist Republican in the tradition of John Maclean and Hugh MacDiarmid, a man Jim knew well. Indeed it was Jim McLean who produced some of the best recordings of MacDiarmid reading his own work. McLean is one of the finest Scottish song-writers in recent years. His

Glencoe, for example, rightly lays the Massacre and the subsequent divisions between Scottish Catholics and Protestants, squarely at the door of William Prince of Orange. King Billy, he suggests (in words that might have come straight from the pen of MacDiarmid or Hamish Henderson) was to be the bane of all Scottish political and cultural development in the centuries that followed. Coming, as he Jim does, from a family steeped at one time in the Orange tradition, he knows well what he's writing about. Living nowadays with one foot in Euston and the other in Glasgow Central, Jim started Nevis Records so as to – literally – give a voice to Scots singers and musicians. He lives in London with his wife and two sons, Calum and Ian.

ADAM McNAUGHTON

...is a well-known Glasgow songwriter and folk singer with the group *Stramash*. Also in this Folk Group is John Eaglesham of the Mitchell Library whom we would like to thank here for time, trouble and courtesy while tracking down for us the Jimmy Tyrie song.

PHIL McPHEE

...lives in Castlemilk. In a note he says: "I remember the humiliation of standing in a separate queue for free dinners at school. My hatred of capitalism and the Establishment started there. I have been put out of work many times for defending the interests of working-class people, and not only against greedy and unscrupulous employers but also against corrupt and incompetent Trade Union representatives. I have been directly involved in most of our local community struggles, and my belief that ordinary people have the capacity to organise and win victories without the leadership of self-appointed gurus has been vindicated a hundred times over."

ANNE MULLEN

...comes from Govan originally. She lived in England for a number of years where she went to find work. She now lives in Ayrshire.

J. N. REILLY

...was born in 1957. Works in line for publication include: *Maybe a Boy, The Pink Book, Triptych, The Fall of Joseph Smith, Magnificent Despair (a mystery story), Sun and Flesh (a love story).* He has published in the Edinburgh Review and in the anthology Behind the Lines.

JANETTE SHEPHARD

...belongs to one of the great ethnic groups of the old Gorbals – the Lithuanians. We know about the Jews (many of whom, of course, were Lithuanian as well as Estonian and Latvian and Russian), the Irish, the Poles and the Italians, but – at least in my memory – the Lithuanians stand out. They had a capacity for friendship and kindly feeling which the harsh conditions of life in the Gorbals did not always make easy. I was privileged to know and have close friendships with two or three unforgettable people from among them. As her grandparents had moved to Scotland in search of a better life, so Janette in her turn moved out of the Gorbals with – as she so movingly portrays it in her fine story *Where I Came From* – a no doubt similar dream. The dreams lie crushed and dead. But what is history but a catalogue of dead dreams that somehow worked a magic beyond their death? What is of value endures. And this will be true for Janette.

BILL SUTHERLAND

...was born and reared in Dumbarton. The poems in this book are extracts from *A Clydeside Lad,* a manuscript in verse about growing up in the working-class culture of Clydeside in the heyday of the shipyards. He is at present employed as Oral Historian for the Scottish Maritime Museum. He has had poems published in Poetry Review, The Tablet and other magazines.

JEFF TORRINGTON

writes: "I see we were both born in the same year and in the same district. I also went down with TB and was cured thanks to streptomycin. My sanatorium was single ward in Shieldhall Fever Hospital. Another curious coincidence is the fact that the main character in my nearly completed novel is called Thomas Clay which must be a further Anglification of your own name. I believe you were handy with the boxing gloves back in the old days when Gorbals was really the Gorbals. I wonder if you remember Roy Ankarah (not sure of the spelling) also known, I think, as the Black Flash. He used to live along in Oatlands and did some of his street work there.

(I remember Roy Ankarah very well. He had a couple of famous fights in London with Al Phillips, the Aldgate tiger. I remember listening in to the radio commentaries. I think Roy had the Empire featherweight title at the time. But the Gorbals was at that time overflowing with boxers, amateur and pro, all sharing the gym space and training and sparring together, one reason the area came up with so many champions and near champions. Vic Herman, who won the British flyweight title and contended for the world title, lived just round the corner from me in Abbotsford Place, and round the corner from him in Kelty

Street was George Lamont who lived with uncle ex-fighter Billy Hood. George's opponent in his first pro outing had been this very same Billy Hood! Everybody knows a fighter has to win in his debut. Putting him in with his uncle to ensure a result was cheeky even for those days. They need not have been so cautious with George Lamont. I saw him in the Kelvin Hall about a year later, round about 1951, having a great victory over – yes, Roy Ankarah.)

Jeff Torrington was born in the Gorbals in 1935. He is married with three grown up children and lives in Linwood. He has had short stories and articles published and broadcast on BBC radio.

JACK WITHERS

...was born in Maryhill. Hand and mind worker most of his life, now just mind, with a corresponding sense of loss. Poems and prose in print, theatre and radio plays produced. His work to be found in Lines Review, Words, Logos, Chapman, Radical Scotland, Voices, Information (Denmark), Westermanns Monatshefte (West Germany), Nuernburger Blaetter (West Germany). Winner of the James Kennaway Screenplay Award.

JAMES D. YOUNG

...is a well-known socialist historian, writer and speaker. When Jim Sillars described him as being to "the Left of Lenin" in the House of Commons in 1977, he was not engaging in flattery. In arguing for socialist ideas during the past forty years Young has addressed countless meetings. A prolific contributor to obscure socialist newspapers and journals in the 1950s, James D. Young is the author of *The Rousing of the Scottish Working Class* (Croom Helm, 1979), *Women and Popular Struggles* (Mainstream, 1985), and *Making Trouble* (Clydeside Press, 1987). He plans to go on making trouble for the capitalist Establishment. He has just completed a pamphlet on *John Maclean and Thatcherism;* and he is working on several books including a history of working-class Glasgow.